Foreword

Welcome

Welcome to this latest in-depth examination of the rolling stock of British Rail and on into privatisation. Previous entries in this series have looked at the BR engineers' wagon fleet in all its diverse forms, so this volume is something of a companion piece as it considers the equally complex world of departmental coaching stock.

As the name suggests, this involves both passenger and non-passenger coaches such as parcels vans that found a second career after withdrawal from revenue-earning work. These new roles were exceptionally diverse, ranging from use as a lowly stores van with no modifications beyond a change of number, to vehicles that were almost completely rebuilt, such as to carry re-railing equipment or serve as work platforms from which maintenance to overhead electrification could be conducted.

Over the decades, thousands of coaches found use in such ways, stretching from pre-grouping and 'Big Four' stock to numerous BR Mk.1s and even some Mk.2s and Mk.3s. As such, it is impossible to cover everything in one volume so the focus here is on coaches that either worked with or complemented the engineers' wagon fleet during the diesel era. As such, the subjects to be found within these pages include the breakdown and electrification stock previously mentioned along with staff, tool and dormitory coaches and vans. Also featured are stores vans, weedkilling trains and the vehicles used to maintain tunnels and viaducts. Naturally, some of these topics also cross into the world of wagons and on-track plant so these are covered alongside where necessary, such as BR's breakdown crane fleet.

With the coming of privatisation, many departmental coaches fell victim to changing working practices or increased health and safety legislation and were withdrawn. However, some lingered on into private ownership for a short time and these again feature in the appropriate sections. Subject to demand, a second volume will hopefully further explore this subject, including the likes of inspection saloons and exhibition trains, and also delve further into the different types of on-track plant. As usual, the prototype analysis is supported throughout by a variety of modelling projects, some of which are simple but others much more in-depth given the often bespoke nature of the vehicles being portrayed.

As ever, this special could not have been produced without the knowledge and assistance of Trevor Mann and David Ratcliffe, who have authored several of the sections. Thanks are also due to Greg Brookes, Tony Buckton, Tom Curtis, Steve Farmer, Mark Lambert, Gary Long, Bob Taylor, Hywel Thomas, Roland Turner and Paul Wade for their input in the modelling sections and to all the photographers that have also contributed.

Simon Bendall
Editor

ABOVE: 'Crompton' 33047 *Spitfire* was outside its normal stomping ground on August 14, 1991, as it passes through Totnes with a westbound engineers' service, probably bound for Tavistock Junction, Plymouth. The leading two vehicles are the primary interest here, the nearest being DB889027, which was originally a 14-ton motor car ferry van to freight diagram 1/291 but now rebuilt into a staff van with new fixed ends along with a revised bodyside door and window layout. These vehicles were sometimes referred to as ferry CCTs due to their strong resemblance to the longer Mk.1 Covered Carriage Trucks, an unidentified example of which is coupled directly behind. A few of these latter vehicles served as tool vans for track machines, such as the Plasser & Theurer RM74 ballast cleaner next along, with the rest of the visible train being YCV Turbot ballast wagons. Simon Bendall Collection

COVER: One of the most commonly seen types of departmental coaching stock were the weedkilling trains. On September 4, 1996, 20901 *Nancy* ambles through Kingham on the Cotswold Line with an Old Oak Common to Hereford working of the distinctive Nomix-Chipman set. Martin Loader

THE GREAT ELECTRIC TRAIN SHOW

LAYOUTS, DEMONSTRATIONS, QUALITY TRADE & MORE!

SAVE THE DATE!

OCTOBER 8/9 2022

Arena MK, Stadium Way, Milton Keynes MK1 1ST

Keep your eye on our website and future *Hornby Magazine* issues for a full list of layouts, updates, demonstrators and exhibitors

Visit us at...
keymodelworld.com/greatelectrictrainshow

Brought to you by...
KEY | HORNBY magazine | KEY MODEL WORLD

Contents

6	A coach for any occasion
10	Big lifts and support
28	Electrifying flat-tops
36	A home from home
58	Stores on the move
74	Inspecting the tunnels
87	Weeding the network
109	Viaduct visualisation

ABOVE: Departmental coaching stock came in pretty much any size, shape, and colour imaginable and, sometimes, it was not even a coach anymore! In many cases though, such vehicles were little different from their as-built condition with only small alterations made for their role with one of the engineering departments. Stores coaches and vans were a particular example of minimalist changes as exemplified by DB977016, a former Mk.1 Full Brake that was part of the Eastern Region weedkilling train and used to carry the chemicals for on-board mixing with water before spraying over the trackbed and lineside. Details of how to build this train in N gauge can be found on pages 91-93.
Tony Buckton

ISBN: 978 1 80282 193 2
Editor: Simon Bendall
Main contributors: Trevor Mann, David Ratcliffe
Senior editor, specials: Roger Mortimer
Email: roger.mortimer@keypublishing.com
Design: SJmagic DESIGN SERVICES, India.
Cover design: Dan Jarman
Head designer: Steve Donovan

Advertising Sales Manager: Brodie Baxter
Email: brodie.baxter@keypublishing.com
Tel: 01780 755131

Advertising Production: Rebecca Antoniades
Email: rebecca.antoniades@keypublishing.com

Subscriptions/Mail Order
Key Publishing Ltd, PO Box 300, Stamford, Lincs, PE9 1NA
Tel: 01780 480404 **Fax:** 01780 757812

Subscriptions email: subs@keypublishing.com
Mail Order email: orders@keypublishing.com
Website: www.keypublishing.com/shop

Publishing
Group CEO: Adrian Cox
Publisher: Mark Elliott
Head of Publishing: Finbarr O'Reilly
Chief Publishing Officer: Jonathan Jackson

Key Publishing Ltd, PO Box 100, Stamford, Lincs, PE9 1XP
Tel: 01780 755131 **Website:** www.keypublishing.com
Printing
Precision Colour Printing Ltd, Haldane, Halesfield 1, Telford, Shropshire. TF7 4QQ
Distribution
Seymour Distribution Ltd, 2 Poultry Avenue, London, EC1A 9PU **Enquiries Line:** 02074 294000.

We are unable to guarantee the bonafides of any of our advertisers. Readers are strongly recommended to take their own precautions before parting with any information or item of value, including, but not limited to money, manuscripts, photographs or personal information in response to any advertisements within this publication.

© Key Publishing Ltd 2022

All rights reserved. No part of this magazine may be reproduced or transmitted in any form by any means, electronic or mechanical, including photocopying, recording or by any information storage and retrieval system, without prior permission in writing from the copyright owner. Multiple copying of the contents of the magazine without prior written approval is not permitted.

A coach for any occasion

The departmental coaching stock fleet encompassed a vast range of vehicles in an equally diverse number of roles. At one end of the spectrum there were the glamorous and mysterious members of the BR Research department, but most were much more mundane although still fulfilling useful roles. Simon Bendall describes the development of the various series over the decades and their subsequent fall from favour.

ABOVE: **In the shadow of the Clifton suspension bridge, the Civil Engineers' depot at Ashton Gate was home to an eclectic mix of departmental coaches and wagons, many associated with the local tunnel inspection train which was responsible for maintaining the Severn Tunnel. In late 1989, a delightfully scruffy 50015 *Valiant* is marshalling this train ready for its next duty with staff coach DW150144 prominent in the formation. This was converted from a Great Western Collett-design 57ft Brake Third Corridor built in 1927 and eventually scrapped in 2004 after the best part of a decade stored at Bristol East Depot. The wagons accompanying it are 12-ton pipes taken into departmental stock and fitted with rudimentary 'festoon' lighting on wooden poles while several stores vans are visible in the background, two being Mk.1 CCTs.**
Simon Bendall Collection

Throughout the existence of the railways, there has always been a need for coaches for purposes beyond carrying passengers, parcels, mail, and other light goods. Termed non-revenue earning, these vehicles could, for example, convey workers to sites of track renewals as well as give them somewhere to rest, eat and sleep on long jobs.

Under the auspices of the 'Big Four' of the GWR, LMS, LNER and SR, sizeable fleets of non-revenue coaches were assembled, some being purpose-built for their roles, but the majority converted from redundant stock. These coaches were sometimes termed 'service stock' but under British Rail, the designation of 'departmental stock' became the preferred term as all the vehicles were assigned to an owning engineers' department that was responsible for their use and maintenance.

These various fleets were very much reliant on 'hand me downs' from revenue use; as new stock entered passenger service, those coaches that were displaced would be offered to the engineers where those taken on would replace even older vehicles in a second career. For modellers, this offers an opportunity to run stock that is generations apart on the same layout.

Under BR, purpose-built departmental stock was rare, being confined to a handful of inspection saloons and a small selection of other vehicles, so the mainstay of its conversions were Mk.1s of many different types. These were taken on in their hundreds for numerous purposes, some seeing virtually no alterations while others were extensively rebuilt as the following chapters will show.

Numbering

Prior to Nationalisation, the numbering of departmental coaches had been chaotic across the four companies. To give some measure of order, the early 1950s saw British Railways introduce regional number series into which vehicles could be re-numbered. For those converted by the Eastern Region, the series from DE320000 onwards was allocated, the 'DE' prefix standing for 'Departmental Eastern', while for the London Midland Region, the numbers ran from DM395001 onwards and the Western Region used the DW150xxx series.

The Southern Region was the last to adopt a new number range in 1957, this being from DS70000 upwards, and as a result it had a number of vehicles, mainly staff and tool vans, in traffic with older haphazard numbers. In fact, none of the new number series were perfect with vehicles remaining outside of them and even after the use of the four ranges ceased in 1971, a few additions were made later in the decade to deal with anomalies.

A coach for any occasion

From 1966, BR introduced a single centralised numbering system for all future departmental coaching stock conversions beginning at DB975000, but this was not fully adopted for another five years. Once this number range became full with the allocation of DB975999 in 1980, the series jumped to DB977000, and this was all but exhausted by the time DB977997 was assigned in 2009. Thereafter, the intention was to use the DB971001 upwards series for departmental coaches but only the first four numbers were issued in 2010 before the practice ceased. Since then, subsequent conversions for the likes of Network Rail test trains have retained their existing numbers, partly due to a more lackadaisical approach to such matters and also the considerable paperwork costs that declaring a vehicle change incur.

The reason for the jump from DB975999 to DB977000 in 1980 was that the DB976xxx series was earmarked for wagons taken into departmental stock that required re-numbering. This series was little used in practice with only some 60 or so numbers issued by BR over the years, this sometimes being due to the wagons having received significant modifications that were far removed from their original purpose. This included vans converted to tunnel inspection wagons as detailed in the relevant chapter in this publication.

Code expansion

With the introduction of the Total Operations Processing System (TOPS) computer in 1973, further codes were progressively applied to departmental coaches to denote certain characteristics. Two of these are worthy of explanation as they indicated ownership and braking types, this being information that is useful to modellers to allow accurate train formations to be assembled if desired.

Starting with ownership, a third letter was added to the number prefix to show which of the various engineering arms each vehicle belonged to, as was also the case with the departmental wagon fleets. For the Civil Engineers, the existing prefix remained unchanged, be it DB, DE, DM, DS or DW, whereas an A was added to the front for those owned by the Mechanical & Electrical Engineers. The other significant prefixes were K for the Signal & Telegraph fleet, L for Electrification and R for the Derby-based Research division. Others were used much more sparingly but have some relevance to vehicles in this volume, these being: C - British Rail Engineering Ltd (BREL) workshops, P - Shipping and International services, T - Traffic, X – Stores, and Z - Public Affairs and Publicity.

Similarly, the three-letter TOPS codes also began to be applied to denote a vehicle's purpose, the first letter almost universally being Q to indicate a departmental coach although some use was also made of Z for selected two or three axle vehicles. The second letter then gave details of the usage, examples being P for staff use, Q for a tool van and R for a stores vehicle, although so diverse were the roles undertaken that these were of limited use in some cases.

Finally, the third letter of the TOPS code showed the type of brakes fitted. In many

ABOVE: **Portraying what could be considered a typical Mk.1 coach in departmental service is KDB977166 at York Leeman Road on May 25, 1987. Now a staff coach for the Signal & Telegraph engineers, this remains recognisable as a former Brake Second Corridor (BSK); indeed, its passenger compartments are still intact as seen through the bodyside windows. Modifications have included the removal of the corridor connections, fitting of a through air brake pipe (hence the QPW TOPS code) and the installation of a generator in the brake area. This would be supplying power to the external solebar lighting as well as any suitably-equipped wagons via the jumper connections on the ends. Initially employed as part of the Project Mercury fleet and later gaining the accompanying light blue livery, it then saw use on the modernisation of the West Coast Main Line under Balfour Beatty ownership (see p.48-49). Today it is owned by the Bluebell Railway and based at East Grinstead to provide passenger amenities.** Trevor Mann

LEFT: **Illustrating the diverse nature of what was considered departmental coaching stock, three very different vehicles appear in this image at Eastleigh depot in 1981. Taking centre stage is Taylor & Hubbard heavy duty steam crane DRT80131 from the Civil Engineers' fleet and its jib runner DS3104, which used the underframe of a LSWR 56ft coach. Already withdrawn at this stage, the crane still survives today in preservation, but the runner was scrapped in 2015. In the centre is the depot's breakdown train support vehicles including ex Southern Parcels & Miscellaneous Van (PMV) ADS70154, which was serving as a tool van and is now preserved at the Mid Hants Railway. With it are former 12-ton pipe wagon ADB741291, demountable tank DB749045 and Protrol EG well wagon ADB901451, which was originally built to carry aircraft propellers. Finally, there is sandite and de-icing EMU 003, formed of ADB975594 and ADB975595, which is stabled on an unelectrified road awaiting the onset of autumn. This was converted from a pair of Class 405 4-SUB motor coaches and scrapped in 2004.** Simon Bendall Collection

A coach for any occasion

ABOVE: BR had a long pedigree of converting goods vans into staff vehicles for use with cranes and other plant, these providing messing and dormitory facilities for operating crews during possessions. Amongst the very last conversions were a pair of 22-ton ferry vans, which were rebuilt at York in 1994, so much so that they bore little resemblance to their original appearance when finished. The extent of the work seemingly justified renumbering the wagons into the BR departmental coaching series, which was a unique occurrence. Wearing a short-lived blue and grey livery and yet to be lettered, LDB977923 with LDB977922 behind stand ex-works at Leeman Road that June. They would be scrapped a decade later, some of this time having been spent in store. *Mark Saunders*

instances, this was vacuum (indicated by a V) given the age of the vehicles usually involved, but sometimes with a through air pipe added for operational flexibility (W). For some major conversion programmes, dual air and vacuum brakes (X) would be provided to allow any loco to haul the stock, such as breakdown trains and overhead line maintenance (OHLM) sets. Air-braked only (A) or air with a vacuum pipe (B) departmental stock was comparatively rare until the late 1980s when increasing numbers of transferred Mk.2 coaches and a decreasing number of vacuum-fitted locos made it a more viable option. Indeed, overhauls of breakdown and OHLM coaches among others in the first half of the 1990s would often see the vacuum brakes removed as they were by now deemed redundant.

Into decline
As the 1990s progressed, the departmental coaching stock fleet entered severe decline. The movement of stores by rail had already ceased as it was cheaper to send the parts by road rather than maintain a dedicated fleet of vehicles. It was the coming of privatisation in the middle of the decade along with other contributing factors that really decimated what remained though.

With BR's various maintenance functions splintered into many companies, selected items of rolling stock passed into their ownership. However, the ever-increasing use of road/rail equipment served to make much of this redundant as such vehicles could conduct inspections of tunnels and viaducts as well as maintenance to overhead electrification. With a network of lineside access points also created by Railtrack and then Network Rail, specially-equipped road vans could provide staff amenities close to worksites, removing the need for staff coaches.

The rapid tightening of health and safety legislation also had a significant effect, the thought of staff sitting in a wooden-bodied van with a gas heater, cylinders in a cabinet beneath and ventilation and emergency exit concerns doubtless inducing a few palpitations amongst officialdom. Similarly, overhead line workers atop flat-topped coaches with an unrestrained fall to the track below came to be similarly frowned upon, quite rightly after numerous incidents over the years. A handful of modernised vehicles from both categories did continue to operate into the early years of privatisation but their use eventually petered out.

In more recent times, working at height legislation effectively spelled the end for Network Rail's Cowans Sheldon breakdown cranes due to the need to climb on various parts to set them up. Finally, in some cases, the departmental coaches were just outright replaced, such as the last weedkilling trains by the Windhoff-built Multi-Purpose Vehicles.

Wagons and cranes
As mentioned in the introduction, some wagons fall into the scope of this special, particularly those vans and brake vans that were converted into staff and dormitory vehicles. These were somewhat rudimentary compared to the comfort of a Mk.1 but served a purpose once their bodywork had been suitably altered with remodelled doors and added windows. In some cases, these wagons remained unfitted (denoted by an O as the third letter in the TOPS code) or were unfitted with a through vacuum pipe (P), although some were fully vacuum-braked.

With engineering cranes having been dealt with in a previous volume in this series, it is the turn of the typically larger breakdown cranes to get some attention. The development of the two types was broadly similar though with examples provided by several manufacturers and of varying lifting capabilities. The early-1980s saw a reduction in the number of cranes deemed necessary as safety standards improved along with conversion from steam to diesel power for those that were retained. Further contraction has since taken place under Railtrack and Network Rail, so much so that the present infrastructure owner only has one heavy-lift crane of its own with additional capacity hired in on the thankfully now rare occasions that it is needed.

RIGHT: The passengers on the 11.50 Glasgow-Nottingham had a lucky escape on July 8, 1977, when train loco 45067 ploughed into an already derailed coal train near Ilkeston. While the virtually new and loaded HBA hoppers were scattered everywhere, the passenger train derailed but remained upright, meaning no significant injuries were incurred. Toton deployed both of its cranes to conduct recovery operations the following day where Cowans Sheldon 36-ton steam crane ADM1106 is seen lifting a mangled wagon with two others still overturned. The crane would soon be renumbered as ADRC95223 and survives today at Peak Rail. *Simon Bendall Collection*

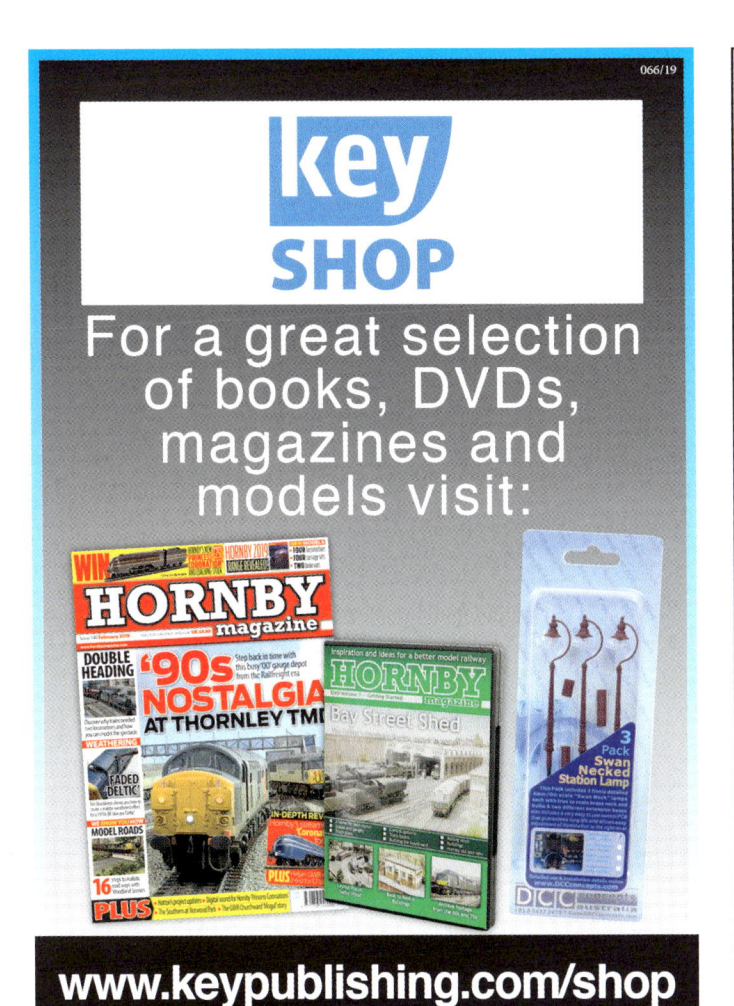

key SHOP

For a great selection of books, DVDs, magazines and models visit:

www.keypublishing.com/shop

066/19

ElectraRail Graphics
electrarail.co.uk
Vinyl overlay and livery specialist

Massive range in OO and N

Easy to apply - peel and stick!

Departmentals a speciality!

See it all at **www.electrarail.co.uk**

E-mail: sales@electrarail.co.uk
Telephone: 07906 148070

Electra Rail
8 Chapel Lane
Orton Waterville
Peterborough
PE2 5EG

www.electrarail.co.uk

Write for Key!

Having established itself as a leading publisher of railway books, Key Books is now looking for authors to join its international team of contributors. We are looking for existing authors and new ones, who really know their subject, especially if they have a great picture collection that could become an illustrated book.

BR: FROM GREEN TO BLUE

CANADIAN PACIFIC IN THE ROCKIES

CLASS 37s

CZECH AND SLOVAK RAILWAYS
THREE DECADES OF CHANGE, 1990–2020s
KEITH FENDER

HIGHLAND RAILWAYS

Key BOOKS

To propose an idea or find out more, simply email
books@keypublishing.com

We look forward to hearing from you!

012/22

Big lifts and support

The Department of Mechanical & Electrical Engineers had a number of cranes under its control, the most notable of which were the breakdown cranes. Accompanied by a wide range of support coaches and wagons, these would attend the scene of major accidents and derailments in order to recover damaged stock and clear the line, as **David Ratcliffe** explains.

Upon Nationalisation in 1948, British Railways had inherited a varied fleet of breakdown cranes with lifting capabilities ranging from 25 to 50 tons. However, as new locomotives continued to increase in size and weight, this fleet was soon in need of modernisation. Consequently, in November 1959 and after consultations with Ransomes & Rapier and Cowans Sheldon, the two main suppliers of breakdown cranes, BR placed an order with the latter firm for ten new 30-ton and 12 new 75-ton cranes.

Delivered in 1961/62, the new cranes were all painted in the Breakdown Train Unit's (BTU) newly introduced bright red livery, while the existing breakdown cranes and their support vehicles, most of which were then in black livery, were scheduled to be repainted red when they received their next major overhaul. Several factors, including reliability and cost, meant that of the 22 cranes ordered in 1959, 18 were steam powered. The other four, two 30-tonners and two 75-tonners, were diesel-mechanical as they were intended for allocation to the largely-electrified Southern Region.

However, the considerable reduction in route miles that followed the implementation of the Beeching Report, together with the introduction of portable Maschinen Fabrik Deutschland (MFD) hydraulically-operated re-railing equipment, reduced the need for breakdown cranes. By the end of the 1960s, some 72 of the older steam breakdown cranes that BR had inherited had been withdrawn. Furthermore, as the number of serious derailments steadily declined in the following decades, the need for a large number of cranes also fell, resulting in more withdrawals over the next three decades.

In 1974, a new numbering system was introduced for on-track plant to replace the various different regional numbering schemes then in use, breakdown cranes being allocated numbers in the 95xxx (steam-powered) and 96xxx (diesel-powered) ranges with the final prefix letter indicating the builder. However, it took several years for the new numbers to be fully applied.

In response to a derailment at Helmsdale, 26039 heads north at Muir of Ord on May 28, 1975, with the Inverness breakdown train. In tow is a Cowans Sheldon 30-ton crane originally built for the LMS in the early 1940s, its boiler already being lit in preparation for use. Also in the consist are the obligatory tool van and staff coach. Simon Bendall Collection

Big lifts and support

ABOVE: Cravens 50-ton crane RS1015/50 (also numbered TDM1015) is seen in action at Weaver Junction on August 10, 1975. Built for the LMS in 1931 and initially allocated to Newton Heath, by 1975 it was based at Allerton and, together with the Crewe and Wigan cranes, had been sent to help clear the line following the infamous 'Whisky & Soda' accident. This had occurred four days earlier when the 21.30 Runcorn Folly Lane Sidings to Wallerscote ICI tank train, carrying 47% caustic soda liquor and hauled by 40189, had run away on the Up Liverpool line and collided with the 18.05 Coatbridge to Southampton Freightliner. This was hauled by 86103 and was passing Weaver Junction on the Up Main at the time. Many of the containers on the Freightliner, which had been loaded with bottles of Scotch whisky, were badly damaged as were nine of the caustic soda tank wagons. These leaked their contents into a nearby pond known as Dutton Flash, requiring an extensive clean-up operation. This crane, which became ADRV95206, would be withdrawn in 1982 and is now at the Keighley & Worth Valley Railway. *David Ratcliffe*

Steam to diesel

Unsurprisingly, the ten new 30-ton cranes delivered in 1961 had proved to be poorly-suited to breakdown work and were soon assigned to other duties. For example, the Southern Region's pair of diesel mechanical 30-tonners found employment with the Power Supply Section at Horsham while, during the 1970s, the rest were sold, either to preserved railways or to the Irish state operator Córas Iompair Éireann (CIE). During the 1980s, the majority of the remaining steam-powered 45 and 50-ton breakdown cranes, all of which had been built prior to 1949, were also gradually withdrawn with the last, ADRR95210, seeing its boiler certificate expire on June 1, 1988.

Meanwhile, between 1976 and 1978, the ten 75-ton Cowan Sheldon steam cranes delivered in 1961/62, ADRC96700-09, had been converted to diesel hydraulic power at Derby Locomotive Works. This work also including the fitting of air brakes, safe load and cant indicators, and radio equipment for communication between the crane driver and the site supervisor, while the engine compartments were also sound-proofed. Repainted in yellow, they were joined in 1977 by a further six new 75-ton diesel-hydraulic cranes which BR had ordered from Cowans Sheldon. However, ADRC96710-15 were built to a new design with telescopic jibs.

Together with the two diesel-mechanical cranes that were already on the Southern Region, this provided a fleet of 18 diesel-powered cranes of 75-ton capacity. This was sufficient to meet the future need for breakdown and recovery duties as well as other operations, such as lifting bridge girders, for which the large capacity cranes were sometimes required.

At the same time, it was also decided to convert five wartime-built Cowans Sheldon 45-ton steam cranes, one of which had already been uprated to 50-tons, to diesel hydraulic power. This work was completed at Derby Locomotive Works during 1985 and the cranes renumbered as ADRC96716-20. Two of these, ADRC96717/20, were later transferred to the Electrification Department but they were not really suitable for this kind of work. By 1994, the pair along with ADRC96716 had been scrapped and the other two sold into preservation.

Further reductions

Early in 1993, it was the turn of the first of the 1961-built 75-ton cranes, ADRC96700, to be withdrawn, while over the next few years, nine more 75-ton cranes would be either sold or scrapped. These included ADRC96711, the Glasgow-based telescopic jib crane, which had seen a reduction in its ballast weights to increase its route availability in Scotland.

Following a Railtrack review in 1997, it was decided that the other five 75-ton telescopic jib cranes would be refurbished and in 1999 they were fitted with new Cummins diesel engines and an enhanced hydraulic system. Improved lighting and cab fittings, including a rear-facing video monitor, were

BELOW: A battered Blue Circle Cement PCA presflo is seen in the course of being re-railed at Cogload Junction, near Taunton, on August 31, 1986. This is being achieved using the MFD system of hydraulic jacks, which slide sideways on their runners to align the vehicle back onto the rails. This system remains in use today and became standard equipment on BR's breakdown trains, allowing minor derailments to be tackled without using a crane. This shot is actually taken at the end of what had been a major recovery operation involving two breakdown units after a cement train from Westbury departed with a handbrake still applied on a wagon, the dragging brakes leading to a severe wheelflat that then struck a check rail on a point, derailing much of the train. *Simon Bendall Collection*

Modelling BR Departmental Coaching Stock 11

Big lifts and support

also installed. Despite its upgrade, within a year ADRC96712 had also been withdrawn with the rail network's subsequent breakdown crane requirement being met by the four remaining telescopic jib cranes, ADRC96710/13/14/15. The fixed jib trio of ADRC96701/02/09 were also retained, either as maintenance cover or for spare parts, before they were also withdrawn between 2006 and 2008.

Three of the remaining telescopic jib cranes were then redeployed to the EWS depots at Bescot, Knottingley and Toton with the fourth kept as a spare at Wigan Springs Branch, although the increasing use of mobile road cranes saw all four going into store at Wigan by 2015. Attempts were then made to make them compliant with new working at height legislation by fitting disfiguring handrails around the weight-relieving bogies but they saw little use in this form. In 2021, ADRC96710 and ADRC96713 were exported abroad while ADRC96714 is preserved at the Gwili Railway and ADRC96715 is currently used by Nemesis Rail at Burton.

In 2016, Network Rail took delivery of a newly-built Kirow heavy-duty diesel-hydraulic crane numbered 99 70 9319 013-7. Although principally for engineering duties, recovery work is well within its capabilities and it has seen such use. If required, Network Rail can also hire three largely identical cranes (DRK81611-13) from Balfour Beatty, Colas Rail and Volker Rail. Indeed, most incidents requiring a heavy lift crane since the mid-2010s have seen one or even two of these Kirow machines attend, effectively bringing the contracting out of recovery work.

LEFT: Until the late 1960s, the breakdown fleet included a number of rather ancient steam cranes such as DE331151, which was built by Cowans Sheldon for the North Eastern Railway in 1916. Based at York until 1963, this 30-ton crane was then transferred to Hull and is pictured at Wath Yard, between Barnsley and Doncaster, in March 1967, some eight months before withdrawal. Its runner wagon was even older than the crane, being a converted well wagon that had been built in 1899! *Trevor Mann Collection*

Prior to the introduction of the red livery, breakdown cranes had been painted black, as seen on 45-ton Ransomes & Rapier example RS1083/45 at what is believed to be Dewsnap Sidings, Manchester, in the mid-1960s. Built in 1943, this crane was initially based at Gorton before being transferred to the London Midland Region in 1960. It was subsequently allocated to Newton Heath in 1965, where it would be renumbered as ADRR95215. It was sold to the Bluebell Railway in November 1981. *Trevor Mann Collection*

Big lifts and support

ABOVE: One of the 12 steam-powered breakdown cranes that remained in use in 1979 was ADRR95201, previously numbered ADS81. Constructed for the Southern Railway in 1927 by Ransomes & Rapier, it had a lifting capability of 36-tons and was recorded, together with its jib runner ADS3088, at Stewarts Lane in December 1980. Given the TOPS code of ZIP, it was eventually withdrawn in February 1986 and subsequently sold to the Kent & East Sussex Railway. Paul Bartlett

ABOVE: Depot open days would sometimes provide the opportunity to photograph a breakdown crane or even see a demonstration of one in action. On such an occasion, Ransomes & Rapier 36-ton steam crane ADRR95225 attracts attention at Eastleigh in May 1983. This crane would be scrapped in 1986 while the last steam-powered breakdown crane was withdrawn from service two years later. David Ratcliffe

ABOVE LEFT: Another steam breakdown crane to be preserved was ADRC95224 (previously numbered ADE330107), which is seen on the North Yorkshire Moors Railway at Grosmont in May 2011. Built by Cowans Sheldon in 1926 and with a lifting capability of 45-tons, this crane was initially allocated to Doncaster before being transferred to Healey Mills in 1965 from where it was sold to the preserved line 1981. Cowans Sheldon would build more breakdown cranes for Britain's railways than all of the other manufacturers combined. David Ratcliffe

ABOVE RIGHT: Another product of Cowans Sheldon, RS1001/50 (later ADRC95202) was an altogether more substantial steam crane, being rated to lift 50-tons and featuring weight relieving bogies either end of the main crane section. Originally built in 1930 for the LMS, it was rebuilt and uprated eight years later and is seen at Wigan Springs Branch on April 28, 1977. This was its final BR depot with sale to the Midland Railway Trust at Butterley coming in 1980, where it still remains today. Simon Bendall Collection

LEFT: Another 50-ton steam crane but this time a product of Cravens would appear to be under test when photographed toying with a 16-ton mineral wagon at Carlisle Upperby in 1976. ADRV95205 (previously RS1013/50), was one of a pair built by the company for the LMS in 1931 and was uprated from 36-tons to 50-tons in 1940. Originally allocated to Rugby, it later spent time at Crewe, Bescot, Longsight and finally Carlisle, from where it was sold to the East Lancashire Railway in 1982. Trevor Mann Collection

Big lifts and support

ABOVE: A spotless Cowans Sheldon 75-ton breakdown crane undergoes testing at Derby in 1965, RS1092/75 having been built three years earlier and recently transferred north from Willesden. These were the pinnacle of BR's steam-powered fleet and would go on to be converted to diesel-hydraulic power at the end of the 1970s, this example becoming ADRC96706. Withdrawn from Toton in 1998, it was initially preserved at the Churnet Valley Railway but was broken up in 2010. Like many steam cranes, the chimney folded down when not in use to keep the crane in gauge. Simon Bendall Collection

ABOVE: As detailed in the text, the Cowans Sheldon breakdown cranes delivered new to the Southern Region at the start of the 1960s were built from the outset with diesel power and mechanical transmission, meaning they were always different to the rest of the fleet, be it in steam form or rebuilt as diesel-hydraulics. One of the two 75-tonners, DB965185, was stabled at Eastleigh on February 2, 1975. Later to become ADRC96200, it was based at Ashford for much of the 1980s and 1990s, being scrapped in 1998. Simon Bendall Collection

ABOVE: Seen at Feltham depot on an unrecorded date in the 1960s is DB965183, one of the Southern's pair of Cowans Sheldon 30-ton diesel-mechanical cranes. Accompanying it are jib runner DB998530, tool van DS70127 and packing material carrier DS70209, which was a former milk tanker underframe fitted with a new, low-sided body. Following the rationalisation of the lower-capacity cranes, this one passed to the Power Supply Section based at Horsham, where, as ADRC96101, it was used for installing transformers for the third rail power supply and other similar jobs throughout the 1980s and early 1990s. Today it is owned by West Coast Railways at Carnforth but is out of use. Simon Bendall Collection

ABOVE: By 1986, the ten diesel-hydraulic Cowans Sheldon cranes that had been converted from steam power were doing most of the work with examples based across the country at Bescot, Crewe, Doncaster, Eastleigh, Gateshead, Holbeck, March, Motherwell, Stratford, and Toton. Following the closure of Gateshead depot in 1991, ADRC96700 was re-allocated to Thornaby and is pictured at Tees Yard in February 1992, a year before it would be withdrawn from service and scrapped by TJ Thomson of Stockton. Like almost all breakdown cranes, it operated with a match wagon which acted as a jib runner and equipment carrier, providing storage for chains and spare lifting tackle. These were often purpose-built and separately-numbered, in this case TDB998541 with the TOPS code of ZSR. David Ratcliffe

LEFT: Both the Crewe and Doncaster breakdown cranes of ADRC96703 and ADRC96709 respectively are seen in action at Chinley on February 22, 1987. Two days earlier, while hauling the 14.32 Peak Forest-Bletchley stone train, 47089 *Amazon* had run away, ending up on its side near Chinley North signal box with some of its de-railed wagons fouling the Up Hope Valley line. These were hit shortly thereafter by 31440, which was heading a Manchester Piccadilly to Sheffield passenger service but, although both locos sustained extensive damage, there were fortunately no serious injuries. After being righted by the breakdown cranes, 47089 was removed to Buxton depot and later taken to Crewe Works where it was deemed to be damaged beyond economical repair and withdrawn. The Class 31 fared no better, being subsequently cannibalised for parts at Doncaster Works. David Ratcliffe

Big lifts and support

ABOVE LEFT: At times, breakdown cranes could be called upon to assist with maintenance work if a location lacked suitable equipment. Seen at Ashford Chart Leacon on March 31, 1992, one end of 47626 is being lifted by ADRC96709 so that a bogie change could take place, the loco having suffered an earlier failure that prevented a return to its home depot. Although based at Ashford at this time, the crane is still lettered for its previous home of Doncaster. Today, ADRC96709 is located at the Great Central Railway and back in its original red livery. Simon Bendall Collection

ABOVE RIGHT: Amusement and bemusement are evident among the passengers as Bruff road/rail recovery lorry C951 YOR arrives at Doncaster in May 1990. These innovative vehicles were introduced by BR at the end of the 1980s to provide a rapid response to incidents, allowing staff and equipment to be quickly brought to a location and removed just as rapidly once done. With a turntable mounted underneath and four-wheel drive, the Bruff would be driven across the tracks, raised-up and aligned, and the rail wheels deployed. Based on a Bedford chassis, equipment carried included hydraulic jacks, cutting gear and an assortment of lighting. This design was progressively withdrawn in the early years of privatisation but DB Cargo today maintains a fleet of four much-larger vehicles based on Volvo lorries. Simon Bendall Collection

LEFT: Illustrating the six telescopic jib cranes built by Cowans Sheldon in 1977 is ADRC96710 at Old Oak Common on August 6, 2000, the occasion of the EWS open weekend. These were considerably more compact machines compared to the earlier fixed-jib cranes and did not require a runner wagon, just weight relieving bogies. Their initial allocations under BR ownership were Bristol Bath Road, Glasgow Eastfield, Old Oak Common, Wigan Springs Branch, Leeds Holbeck and Carlisle Kingmoor. However, initial operational problems meant that they were only used for training until powered outriggers could be provided and they did not enter full service until 1980. This particular example is seen following its refurbishment for Railtrack and displays the company's logos on both the jib and main bodywork. All have now been withdrawn from service with Network Rail, this example being exported in 2021. Simon Bendall

LEFT: Network Rail now only has one heavy-lift crane on its books, this being 125-tonne Kirow KRC1200UK diesel-hydraulic 99 70 9319 013-7. Delivered in March 2016, it is a multi-purpose crane so can be utilised on both engineering and recovery work as needed. On February 6, 2021, it was recorded in transit at Hawkeridge Junction, near Westbury, with its four EWS-liveried FCA support wagons. Of these, 610099 runs empty, 610100 carries the crane's lifting beams and a generator set for lighting, 610314 is loaded with the sizeable counterweight and another generator while 610313 sports workshop and storage containers. All three of the loaded wagons also have safety railings installed around the deck. Steven Clements

Big lifts and support

Improving the Hornby breakdown crane by Gary Long

Although the Hornby model of the Cowans Sheldon steam breakdown crane is regarded by many as toy-like, it can be improved with additional detailing as well as altered to represent a diesel-powered conversion. The main compromise centres around the jib length which is some 30mm too short in order to traverse the tight curves typically found on trainsets, which in turn means the jib runner wagon is too short as well.

I tried a modified extended jib on the crane using articulation at the base, as per the full-size versions, in order to minimise the movement when running around curves. However, this did not suit my layout and visually resulted in the jib being out of alignment with the crane body when returning to straight track. Therefore, I have accepted the underscale nature of the jib and runner and detailed the rest of the crane as best as possible around this compromise.

The crane chassis was left largely unaltered but with a few tweaks to the moulded detail to improve the appearance, such as adding retracted representations of the stabiliser legs. The additional ballast weights on top of the chassis were added using curved plastic, which also have the benefit of stabilising the crane body when it is rotated. These weights were added to the actual cranes to counteract the reduction in weight when the steam boiler and associated ancillary components were removed. The main gear between the top of the chassis and the underside of the body was also added, although I fixed this to the underside of the body as it was more stable in this configuration.

Body modifications

The crane body was modified by adding the operating cab and various other details from plastic sheet and sections. Brass mesh was used for the grilles on the engine compartment with door handles fabricated from thin brass wire. The Hornby operating mechanism for the jib was completely removed and new parts formed from plastic sections and other spare parts. Although not motorised, the winches can be operated from outside the body using a screwdriver in the external bolt head. The pipework and details on the body were added as best as possible based on photos to hand at the time.

Modifications to the runner included reducing the width of the jib support trestle slightly to better match the prototype while a recess was created in the floor to accept the end of the jib. The toolboxes were added below the floor but as the wagon is under length, there was only space for two as opposed to four.

The two weight relieving bogies were designed to distribute the load across a larger area when lifting. These were fixed in the vertical direction but free in the lateral direction when travelling. They were then locked in all directions when lifting but, if not needed, could also be removed, and lifted out of the way prior to recovery operations.

ABOVE: The new winding gear fitted in place with the rigging and pulley wheels along with the lifting hook all being scratchbuilt. Externally, the gearwheel beneath the body and the other details were 3D-printed.

BELOW: The pulleys were made from varied sizes of brass washers glued together around a spindle and then filed to create more of a vee groove. However, a problem arises when moving the jib or crane hook as the rope travels in opposite directions on each adjacent pulley. These will be replaced with small root pulleys purchased from Nigel Lawton 009 which, as separate pulleys, will be able to rotate in different directions and hopefully be more suitable when raising and lowering the jib. The derricking tackle and frames at the bottom were built from square brass section soldered together; these hold the main pulleys to raise and lower the jib.

ABOVE: The crane body is shown with the operator's cab in the process of being created while the roof over the winding gear lies alongside. This is formed from thin brass sheet to match the roof profile and strengthened with strips of plastic ribbing.

Big lifts and support

The slightly unusual coupling pin on these is Hornby's attempt at representing the solid connections between the crane sections but these can affect the running.

Finishing was done using Railmatch post-1984 warning yellow while all of the transfers, including the black stripes, were produced using Corel Draw and printed on clear transfer paper in a laser printer. Buryvale is the name of the fictional depot on my layout and all my engineering trains carry this allocation.

ABOVE: **The lifting hook was cut from a piece of 2.5mm thick mild steel, this coming from a spare wagon weight, and ensured it would have enough weight to hang properly from the thread that was representing the winding cables. The remainder of the assembly was formed from sections cut from flat brass which were then soldered together. The image also shows one of the pulley wheels with the groove filed around the circumference.**

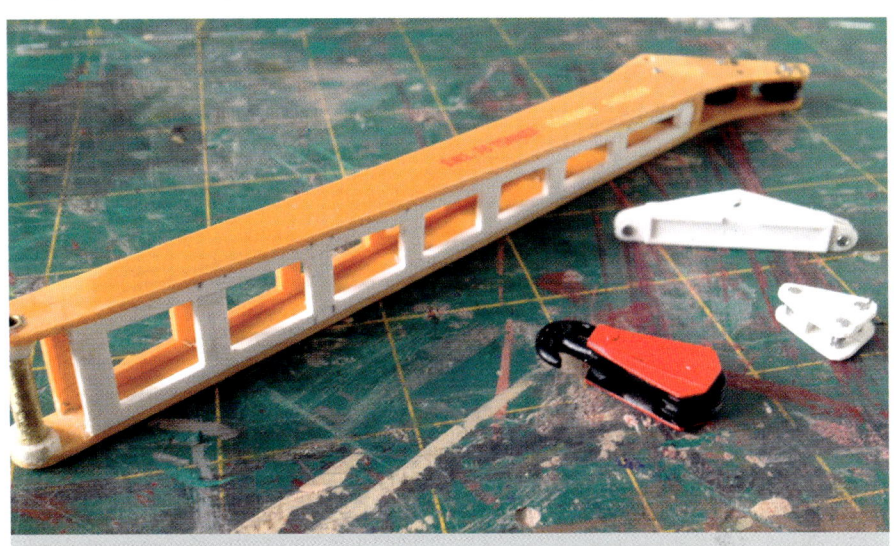

ABOVE: **The jib requires bracing to be added to the underside, this having been omitted by Hornby, presumably to make the moulding process easier. The spreader beam and other lifting components are formed using sections cut from plastic sheet with metal pins added.**

ABOVE: **The engine compartment shows the alterations necessary to represent a diesel-power crane with access doors added and the reprofiled roof to match the section over the winding gear. One of the additional ballast weights on the chassis can be seen beneath the cab along with steps and solid buffer blocks made from plastic.**

ABOVE: **The end of the jib has received the new red-painted derricking tackle/frame along with pulleys, these being secured with a mix of brass pins and small brass countersunk bolts.**

ABOVE: **The weight relieving bogies have gained new etched ladders while the moulded lifting eyes were also cut off and replaced with metal banjo tags with the tags cut short. These were then folded at an angle and glued in place. Meanwhile, the jib runner shows its deck recess and underframe toolboxes, this also receiving new steps and added handrails on the ends. Lifting eyes were also created using the same method as the bogies.**

ABOVE: **Although still under scale length, the alterations made to the Hornby crane have elevated it far beyond the basic model. Finishing touches on the crane chassis included removing the moulded handwheels and steps in favour of etched items from the spares box, while the rigging was replicated using black linen thread.**

Modelling BR Departmental Coaching Stock **17**

Big lifts and supports

BTU Coaches and Wagons

ABOVE: Engineering work at Clapham Junction on October 20, 1984, has necessitated the presence of two steam breakdown cranes to work in tandem. While the water tank for the nearest crane has remained attached, the ex-Southern support coaches have been drawn clear of the worksite. 73119 resides in the station's platforms with one set while the red end of the other can just be glimpsed in the distance. Simon Bendall Collection

In addition to modernising the fleet of breakdown cranes, BR also eventually decided to phase out the use of pre-nationalisation coaches as breakdown train unit (BTU) staff and tool vehicles and gradually replace them with modified Mk.1 stock. However, some of these older vehicles would remain in BTU service until 1986 as a lack of funds meant that the conversion programme for the replacements was undertaken in fits and starts. As with the pre-nationalisation coaches, the Mk.1s were converted into either staff coaches, which were furnished with catering and washing facilities, or into tool vans that were used to carry packing and other equipment such as jacks and slings.

In 1984/85 as part of phase two of this modernisation programme, some 32 Mk.1 tool vans were also equipped with an onboard diesel generator, which provided electricity for lifting, lighting, heating, and cooking when the trains were working in locations without an outside power supply. In addition, all 87 Mk.1 BTU coaches (20 staff coaches, 15 staff and tool coaches, 32 tool and generator vans, and 20 tool vans) received updated electrics and any that were not already dual-braked had air brakes installed alongside the vacuum.

Rationalisation

However, the withdrawal of so many breakdown cranes during the 1990s meant that the majority of these refurbished Mk.1s had a relatively short life, with several being sold to preserved lines. Then in 1997, Railtrack's strategic review identified a need for just 17 BTU coaches, with six staff coaches, six tool and generator vans, and five tool vans subsequently receiving another major overhaul at RFS Doncaster. Each of the five active breakdown cranes was assigned three of the overhauled Mk.1s as support vehicles, while the remaining two coaches were used to form a re-railing train based at Allerton, which operated without a crane but with the MFD hydraulic jacks available.

By 2010, several of these overhauled support coaches needed replacement so four Super GUVs, which had been surplus since the end of mail traffic, were transferred from EWS to Network Rail for use as tool vans. Recoded on TOPS as QQA, they were repainted in all-over yellow and renumbered as ADB971001-04. At the same time, Mk.1s ADB975464 and ADB975486, which had previously been in use as support vehicles with the Network SouthEast snowblower machine, were also refurbished for use with the breakdown cranes.

This much reduced fleet of nine vehicles was completed by the overhauled Mk.1 trio of tool and generator van ADB975087 and staff coaches ADB975471 and ADB975477. Initially based at Bescot, Knottingley and Warrington, the fate of these three trains has mirrored that of the Cowans Sheldon telescopic jib cranes with recent years seeing long periods of inactivity at Wigan and Warrington. However, while the cranes have gone, the coaches remain on Network Rail's books for now, their yellow livery being extremely faded and shabby.

Big lifts and supports

ABOVE: Two or three support coaches would usually accompany a breakdown crane to an incident, these carrying equipment and tools as well as providing the staff with mess and sometimes dormitory facilities. Until the mid-1980s, many of the staff coaches and tool vans based on the Southern Region were former Southern Railway vehicles with staff coach ADS70121, previously Maunsell-design Corridor Composite S5595S, being recorded at Selhurst in September 1980. At this time, it formed part of the Southern's relief breakdown train and carries a QQV TOPS code instead of the correct QPV. David Ratcliffe

ABOVE: Also part of the Southern's relief breakdown train was tool van ADS70125, which is seen at Selhurst on September 21, 1980. Converted in 1962 from S3677S, a Corridor Brake Third built at Eastleigh in 1929, all its original doors and windows have been plated over and new large sliding doors fitted on each side for equipment access, such features being typical of tool vans. Ventilation grilles were also added at one end where a small diesel generator was situated and, like ADS70121, it has been painted in the then relatively new yellow livery with black warning stripes. Simon Bendall Collection

ABOVE: Several Southern Railway two-axle parcels vans also found further use as BTU tool vans, including QVW ADS70154. This was converted in 1961 from S2213S, a PMV built at Ashford in 1935. Pictured at Eastleigh in April 1983, this vehicle was later preserved at the Mid-Hants Railway. Trevor Mann

ABOVE: From the Western Region fleet, DW150310 had been converted from a Fruit C just over two years earlier when recorded at Hereford on August 2, 1964. This was used to carry packing material and after transfer to Ebbw Junction was scrapped at Wednesbury in 1972. Simon Bendall Collection

RIGHT: The Windsor lines side of Clapham Junction plays host to another BTU on September 27, 1986, with 73140 having the Wimbledon set in tow. Leading the formation is staff, tool and generator coach ADS70133, staff coach ADS228 and tool van ADS227 with Cowans Sheldon diesel-mechanical crane ADRC96201 bringing up the rear. All three of the coaches initially survived withdrawal from traffic and ADS70133 is still at the Pontypool and Blaenavon Railway while the other two went to the Kent & East Sussex. However, ADS228 was cut in 2000 while ADS227 lost its body to fire damage 11 years later with the remainder going in 2019. Simon Bendall Collection

Modelling BR Departmental Coaching Stock 19

Big lifts and supports

ABOVE: **Staff riding van ADE320607 was converted in 1958 from E41555E and once formed part of the Holbeck breakdown train. A former Great Northern Railway coach built at Doncaster in 1912, it was over 70 years old when recorded awaiting disposal at Tinsley Yard on March 11, 1984.** Trevor Mann

ABOVE: ADE320610 was a tool and packing van converted in 1958 from E62482E, an ex-Great Eastern Corridor Brake Third built in 1920. Formerly part of the Wath breakdown train, it was also at Tinsley awaiting its fate in November 1984 but would survive into preservation at the Colne Valley. Trevor Mann

ABOVE: Built in 1929 as a Gresley-design Restaurant First, ADE320921 looks somewhat incongruous in BTU yellow at Doncaster on September 1, 1981, when serving as a staff and tool coach. At some point in its life, it had also been modified with Mk.1 style window frames, an alteration that was not unknown on former LNER vehicles. Although sold off by BR in 1989, a partly fire-damaged body ensured it was always at risk and it was broken up for spares in 2001. Simon Bendall Collection

ABOVE: Originally a Gresley Brake Third Corridor built at Doncaster in 1926, ADE320692 had been modified for use as a tool van with the Perth breakdown train. A small hoist had previously been fitted to the end platform but when recorded at Perth station in May 1993, it was out of service and awaiting transfer to the internal user fleet. David Ratcliffe

ABOVE: **Withdrawn in the early 1990s was QQV tool van ADB975055, an LNER Thompson Full Brake built in 1946 and previously numbered E70584E. After conversion to a BTU coach, it was based at Thornaby depot but by April 1993, it was to be found in nearby Tees Yard awaiting disposal, which came the following year.** David Ratcliffe

Big lifts and supports

ABOVE: A number of former LMS coaches were to be found in the London Midland Region's breakdown trains, including QPV staff coach ADM395757, which had been converted in 1962 from Brake Third Corridor M5243M. It retained its red livery, first introduced for breakdown train vehicles in 1959, when photographed at Carlisle London Road on August 14, 1981. Trevor Mann

ABOVE: Former parcels vans made for good conversions to tool vans with minimal work required. Still, six-wheel Stove R 32998 was a more unusual choice to join the Tinsley BTU as DB975249, which is seen at Chesterfield on August 22, 1976. Initially preserved at Butterley in 1984, today only the underframe exists beneath a vintage coach body. 53A Models of Hull Collection/David R Vickers

ABOVE: The breakdown train based at Ayr on the west coast of Scotland included some further unusual choices for its formation. Seen at home on September 30, 1981, is ADB975241, the tool van being a former LMS General Utility Van. Dating from 1935, it survives today at the Doon Valley Railway but is in poor condition. Simon Bendall Collection

ABOVE: Perhaps the most luxurious BTU staff coach ever, former LMS inspection saloon ADM45036 was another member of the Ayr set and is also seen on September 30, 1981, at the Scottish depot. Although sold into preservation in 1989, its has not enjoyed a happy life since, becoming increasingly derelict before the body was destroyed in an arson attack at Chinnor in 2012, leaving just the underframe awaiting potential re-use. Simon Bendall Collection

LEFT: The Scottish Region's spare BTU staff and tool coach ADB975077 is seen at Grangemouth depot on August 16, 1981. Converted from Mk.1 BCK 21018, the conversion was rather more basic than what would follow in later years. It was scrapped in 1992, having been based at Fort William for its final years. Trevor Mann

RIGHT: Another early Mk.1 BTU conversion, tool van ADB975088 was residing in Carnforth Bottom End Sidings in August 1981, its red livery having rather faded to pink. This was converted from BSK 34132 and is seen again in a couple of pages time as part of the Motherwell set. Trevor Mann

Modelling BR Departmental Coaching Stock **21**

Big lifts and supports

ABOVE: Originally built for creosote traffic, several of the fleet of BR 22-ton tankers were later re-deployed as water carriers for steam cranes. Previously based at Ashford, ADB998991 is seen at Chesterton Junction in November 1994 after withdrawal. *David Ratcliffe*

ABOVE: Another design to find use as a water tank for steam-powered breakdown cranes was this former demountable beer tank. Recoded as a ZRW, ADB749045 was part of the Eastleigh-based BTU set when photographed in April 1983. *Trevor Mann*

ABOVE: Several special wagons were allocated to BTU use as equipment carriers. Lowmac EQ ADE230956 is seen at Eastleigh in October 1987 having been modified as a coach bogie carrier, although incorrectly coded as a YVW instead of ZVW. *David Ratcliffe*

ABOVE: At least two of the Protrol bogie well wagons built specifically to carry aircraft propellers were eventually allocated to the BTU for use as equipment carriers. YVP ADB901453, the Protrol EF, was photographed at Stewarts Lane in August 1980. *Trevor Mann*

ABOVE: Many of the BR-built fish vans found second careers in departmental service, including 87885 as Barrow Hill-based BTU tool van ADB975419, where it is seen in June 1979. Later transferred to Tinsley, it survives at the Colne Valley. *Simon Bendall Collection*

ABOVE: Two BR-built 12-ton banana vans made up the remainder of the Ayr BTU set, ADB881653 and ADB882074, the latter seen in the appropriate colours at Ayr on September 30, 1981. These were from the final batch to diagram 1/246. *Simon Bendall Collection*

ABOVE: Built to diagram 1/462, pipe wagon ADB741291 had been fitted with a through air pipe for use in the Eastleigh BTU when seen in April 1983. This could be used to transfer materials to a site or carry detached parts from recovered stock. *Trevor Mann*

ABOVE: Some vehicles' time in departmental use was short, such as LMS Stanier BG M31121M, which became BTU tool van ADB975575 in 1976. By October 5, 1980, it was condemned at Swindon Works, having not even received a coat of yellow. *Simon Bendall Collection*

Big lifts and supports

RIGHT: For many, the red and blue scheme is inexorably linked with the Research Department's stock based at the Railway Technical Centre at Derby. However, when it was first created in 1970, it was intended as a wider departmental livery. As a result, a number of early Mk.1 conversions to breakdown vehicles were finished in the colours, including tool van ADB975148, which is seen at Landore depot, Swansea, in October 1974. Another issue that sometimes occurred with departmental coaches was the application of incorrect numbers and this was the case here with the former BSK identified as ADB97515. To the right is sister BTU vehicle ADB975082. Simon Bendall Collection

LEFT: During the 1980s and with more use being made of lightweight jacking and re-railing equipment, some BTUs either lost their cranes or could be deployed without them if the incident was minor enough. It was the latter case in April 1985 as 37154 brings the Bristol BTU through Temple Meads and back onto Bath Road. This consists of QPX staff and tool coach ADB975472 (formerly BSK 35079), tool van ADB975615 (ex BG 80951) and ADB975485, a tool and generator coach converted from BSK 34594. The shorter Mk.1 BG had been re-purposed from its original role as an Enparts coach for HST spares some two years earlier but had yet to be rebuilt to remove all the original doors and windows in favour of just two sliding doors. Simon Bendall Collection

Carlisle Upperby's breakdown train tool van ADB975499 (ex BSK 34365) is seen at Carlisle London Road on August 14, 1981. This is one of the tool vans that, four years later, would be fitted with an onboard generator to power the train's systems. Trevor Mann

In 1985, tool van ADB975088 was one of the 32 BTU Mk.1 coaches to be refurbished, being fitted with dual brakes, new electrical equipment, external lighting, and a diesel generator. Recoded QQX, it was recorded at Motherwell depot in July 1990. David Ratcliffe

The second tool van allocated to Motherwell was ADB975162, which is also seen at the depot in July 1990. These tool vans had strengthened floors covered with chequer-plate to withstand carrying lifting gear and other heavy equipment. David Ratcliffe

Like most staff vans, Motherwell's ADB975467 was fitted out with crew lockers, a drying room and a kitchen area equipped with a cooker, fridge, and sink. One seating compartment was retained with a shower and wash basins also installed. David Ratcliffe

Modelling BR Departmental Coaching Stock

Big lifts and supports

RIGHT: One of the final duties for a Network Rail BTU came in August 2017 following the derailment of a GB Railfreight intermodal at Ely. Cowans Sheldon crane ADRC96715 was dispatched from Wigan Springs Branch along with the former Bescot support coaches of ADB975471, ADB971001 and ADB971003. DRS provided 68016 *Fearless* to power the initial Wigan to Crewe leg then the 4K97 16.03 Basford Hall-Toton on August 15, which has just joined the West Coast Main Line at Basford Hall Junction. The BTU would move on to Whitemoor Yard that evening behind GB Railfreight's 66769. The railings added to the weight relieving bogies of the crane to comply with working at height legislation are plainly evident.
Ian Tunstall

ABOVE: With its yellow livery now heavily faded, QQA ADB971003 stands at the rear of Bescot depot on June 22, 2013. This was one of four Super GUV mail vans taken on by Network Rail in 2010 as replacement BTU tool vans, sister vehicle ADB971003 also being fitted with a generator set and external ventilation grille. Other modifications included the addition of solebar lighting and end electrical connections. This BTU is now stored at Wigan Springs Branch. Dan Adkins

ABOVE: Five of the mid-1970s Mk.1 BTU conversions were retained by Network Rail to work with the four new Super GUVs. Joining ADB971001 and ADB971003 in the Bescot set was staff and tool coach ADB975471, which was originally a BSK and is seen amongst the other residents of the Birmingham depot on October 15, 2015. Now finished in Network Rail yellow, it carries DB Schenker branding in addition to Network Rail logos and is coded QPA. Dan Adkins

Ready-to-run breakdown coach models

Over the decades, a number of breakdown coach models have been produced in RTR form, particularly in 4mm scale, but these have very much resided at the toy end of the market and usually fictitious in nature. Only in recent years have more accurate offerings appeared, starting out as retailer commissions but increasingly as part of manufacturers' main ranges. However, given the bespoke nature of the real BTU coaches, the models invariably do not reflect any of the physical alterations, except by using printed detail at times, such as for grilles and vents. Those based on parcels stock tend to be the most realistic whereas those using passenger Mk.1s are the most compromised.

LEFT: Graham Farish Mk.1 CCT finished as Cardiff Canton tool van ADB977076.

ABOVE: Eastfield's ADB977155, a tool van converted from a Mk.1 BG, which is a Bachmann limited edition currently available from Kernow Model Rail Centre.

LEFT: Hornby has produced its 4mm Super GUV in Network Rail yellow twice to represent Bescot vehicles ADB971001 and ADB971003.

HORNBY magazine

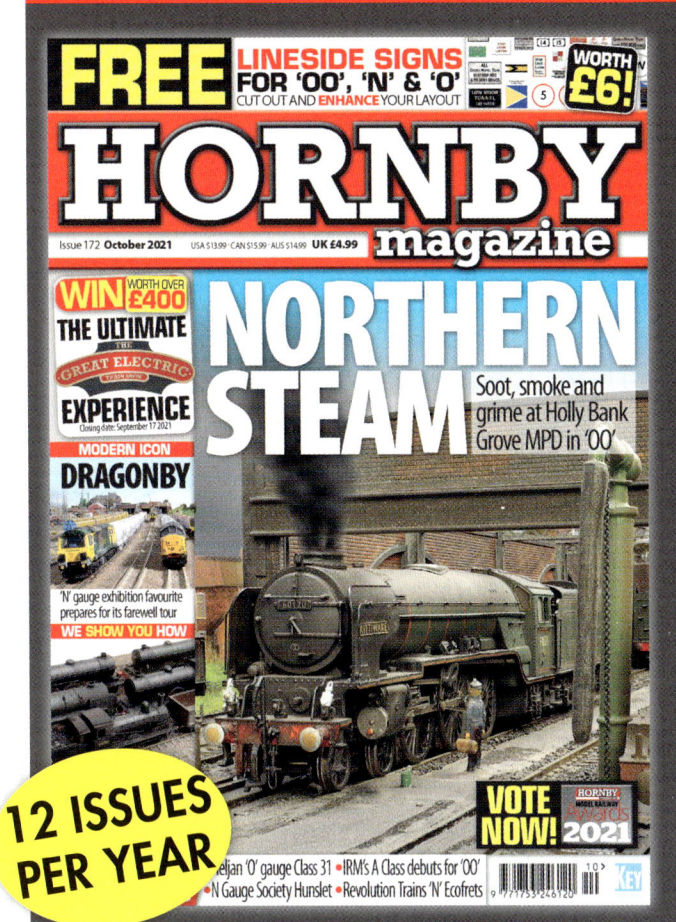

Published monthly in print and digital format and featuring exclusive Hornby Hobbies content, Hornby Magazine takes a unique approach to model railways with both the relatively inexperienced and the seasoned modeller in mind.

Unique step-by-step guides offer modellers hints and tips on how to get the most from the hobby. The very best photography and all the very latest news inspire and inform modellers of all abilities. Hornby Magazine is produced independently, under license from Hornby Hobbies, and is dedicated to promoting this most rewarding of hobbies, introducing it to newcomers and those returning to the hobby. It is written by enthusiasts for enthusiasts - the editorial and publishing team are all active modellers who care passionately about the hobby.

12 ISSUES PER YEAR

KEY MODEL WORLD

Have you visited?
It's your **NEW** online home for railway modelling.
Visit **www.keymodelworld.com** today!

HORNBY magazine

FOR OUR LATEST SUBSCRIPTION DEALS VISIT:

shop.keypublishing.com/hmsubs

+44 (0)1780 480404

383/21

Big lifts and support

Southern Pride BTU coaches by Mark Lambert

The Southern Pride staff coach finished as Toton's ADB975465.

Southern Pride Models produced a large range of coaches and multiple units in 4mm scale, mainly Mk.1-based, and it was a bit of a shame that most of the range disappeared almost overnight when the standard coach roof moulding became unavailable. The kits are multi-media, containing plastic, brass, and whitemetal components and usually come with bogies and wheels.

I had bought two Toton-based breakdown train coaches branded as Etchmaster kits, where instead of the usual pre-painted and self-adhesive vinyl sides, the coach sides are etched brass with self-adhesive window frames. For one of the vehicles, the tool van, this is possibly overkill as there are no windows remaining and only four small generator grilles grouped at one end. I built the coaches as a pair, with tension lock couplings at the inner ends and scale couplings and pipework at the outer ends.

Southern Pride kits have a sort of slot-together design to align the sides, ends and floor but the floor channels that the sides slot into are not fully formed, so it takes a while to prepare the main parts for assembly, cutting and filing the slot clear in the floor moulding. Once the floor is properly cleared, assembly of the main components takes just a few minutes.

I took slightly longer with the staff coach though as, while regular Southern Pride coaches have clear plastic sides, the instructions for the Etchmaster coaches suggest removing a strip of clear material where the windows are, fitting the sides, painting the coach and then refitting the glazing strip. It just seemed so much easier to build the coach complete and glue the painted sides on.

This generally worked well; I added all the door furniture and handrails before giving the sides an undercoat in white and a sprayed topcoat of Army Painter 'Demonic yellow'. One coat provides a bright, slightly sickly yellow but a second application deepens the shade and comes close to a slightly faded BTU yellow. This did mean that I had to mask the clear parts to paint the coach ends in situ, but it was still a lot easier to do than the suggested route.

Adding the detail

I applied all the roof details and then painted the roof separately before fitting it; likewise the end details that were required were also added before the main assembly and painting. Afterwards, the toilet filler pipes were put in place on the staff coach.

BTU coaches often had extra or unusual equipment boxes on the underframe and these two were no exception. Some of the parts were provided as fold-up brass etches, others as plastic mouldings that needed modification. There are a few pictures online of the coaches from my modelling period (over 30 years ago now), which were helpful in identifying which boxes were present and where they went, along with some unusual pipework on the ends of the tool van.

I fitted the fold-up brass parts over the top of some spare plastic underframe boxes so that I could glue them to the underframe more easily and to make the end result more solid. Extra details in the form of cabinet handles and access steps were added as needed, based on the photos. The equipment boxes obscured a lot of the underframe but not where the dual brake equipment was, so a complete set of tanks, distributors and cylinders were required on both coaches. The 'V' hangers, shafts and pulls of the brake equipment are brass and soldered for strength.

The underframes received a coat of Army Painter 'Hardened Carapace' for a clean but in-service look. Southern Pride produces a small sheet of transfers for these coaches while Fox Transfers offers the characteristic black stripes and, for good measure, I also used some Railtec decals to finish the coaches as close to the desired late 1980s/early 1990s period as I could get.

Also from the Toton BTU is tool and generator van ADB975491.

Big lifts and support

Buffing up a Bruff by Gary Long

The Bruff road/rail recovery vehicles were used for the re-railing of rolling stock throughout the 1980s and into the mid-1990s. Around 30 were built with some still surviving on preserved lines and, in addition to carrying jacking equipment, each had its own generator along with air and hydraulic connections to power the jacks. On the cab roof, the strange dustbin-shaped object was a telescopic floodlight, although photos of this extended are rare.

Having built and motorised a Kibri road/rail excavator some years ago, I fancied making my own model of a Bruff and powering it as well. For this I decided to use the motorised chassis from Bachmann's HO scale rail detector step van, which has a wheelbase quite similar to that of the Bruff. The main advantage of using this chassis is that it has small replica rail wheels already fitted, although, as I found out later, these wheels are used for the electrical pick-up for the motor.

As much of the body is square and relatively easy to build, I developed a set of brass etches for the back of the cab and also the box body. The rest of the cab was a bit of an issue as the Bruff used the Bedford TL lorry cab. As this was not available at the time, I used a Bedford TK cab taken from a diecast EFE model, which is close enough in design to be acceptable. The underslung turntable was not modelled as the chassis block is in the way, but a static version complete with turntable may follow at some stage.

Assembly

Taking the EFE lorry, the cab was cut down to suit while the interior and wheels were also retained for re-use. To connect the cab and body to the chassis, a flat etched brass mounting plate was used, this being folded to create a saddle that sat over the entire chassis and has the road wheels attached to it. These do not turn but serve to hide the original rail wheels of the Bachmann donor, which still power the model when it is on the track.

ABOVE: The finished Bruff in rail mode, the small rail wheels being from the donor chassis and function as pick-ups with the larger rail wheels largely obscured behind the road tyres.

ABOVE: The EFE cab with the brass etch for the crew body grafted onto it but with the roof still to be finished.

The etch forming the rear of the cab was folded and soldered together with a flat section soldered on top to create the rain strip around the roof. A small section of plastic sheet was then glued to the roof and profiled to complete the look. The etched box body was assembled in the same way, this incorporating the rear roller shutter door, while an internal supporting structure gave strength along with a fixing on which the cab was attached with epoxy glue.

The bumpers, light bar, grille, and steps were all made of etched brass, which were soldered together and then added to the cab. As part of the etched sheet, I managed to produce the light bar and grille badge with the words Bruff and Bedford proud of the background. The idea was to paint these, picking out the letters separately. When it came to this though, it did not work very well so the lettering was omitted and replaced by transfers. I used modeller's licence on the hydraulic connections at the front as these would normally be covered when travelling but I decided to leave the cover off so you could see the detail.

Lessons learned

I did make a few errors that I would correct on future models. Looking at various photos, I may have been better swapping the front and rear hubs as the Bruff had a strange wheel arrangement when compared with a road-going Bedford truck. I doubt I would get them off now without damaging them. Additionally, the front and rear railway running lights are etched discs which I fixed on and then highlighted after spraying the whole model yellow. This does not give the best results and they would have been better painted off the model and glued on later. I would also consider using the Road Transport Images cab for a Bedford TL (reference BED08), which was not available at the time the model was built.

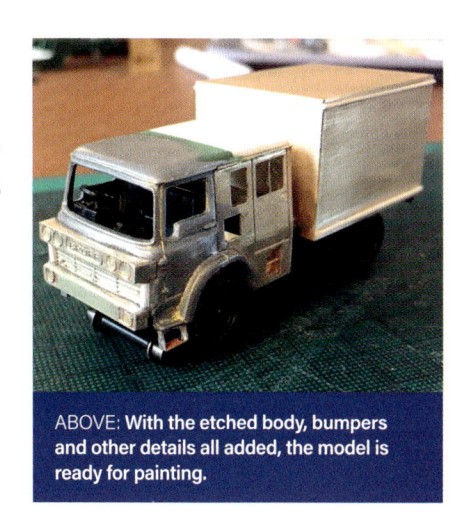

ABOVE: The Bachmann HO chassis with the etched brass mounting plate on top, this having the tyres already attached and ready to receive the cab and body.

ABOVE: With the etched body, bumpers and other details all added, the model is ready for painting.

Modelling BR Departmental Coaching Stock

Electrifying flat-tops

Right from the earliest years of overhead electrification, redundant coaches with their roofs cut flat were used to maintain the wiring. Simon Bendall **explores the vehicles employed by British Rail since the days of West Coast electrification.**

Following the electrification of the Newport to Shildon line by the North Eastern Railway in 1915, companies opting to employ overhead wires frequently adopted a practice of using redundant coaching stock to conduct installation, repair, and maintenance work. The conversions invariably involved the removal of the existing curved roofs and installation of flat replacements, this provided an elevated work platform from which the contact and support wires, insulators, registration arms and other parts could all be accessed relatively easily, using additional ladders if needed.

Access to the flat roofs could be made by external ladders or internal steps through roof hatches while bridging plates between coaches gave uninterrupted access along the train. Unsurprisingly, working at this height on a relatively narrow surface and without restraints came with risks, especially in a time before safety became prevalent, so falls resulting in injuries or even fatalities were not unknown.

Under British Railways, the existence of the electrified Woodhead route over the Pennines as well as the growth of an assortment of suburban networks ensured that both the Eastern and London Midland regions had a considerable number of maintenance coaches among their regional fleets. As well as the flat roof, these would typically see extensive rebuilding of the rest of the bodywork, altering and reducing the number of windows, adding large sliding access doors, and reconfiguring the ends to remove gangway connections if fitted to create access doors. Mesh screens over the windows protected them from damage by falling parts and also served as useful anti-vandal protection for stock that could be inactive in sidings for lengthy periods.

Formed into trains of five or so vehicles, the coaches had a variety of roles, such as providing workshop areas, materials and tool storage, office space and staff facilities. One coach would be fitted with a generator to power the train's systems, this including the external lighting installed along the edges of the flat roofs, while another would feature a pantograph at one end that could be raised, unpowered, to assess the height and positioning of the contact wire. Completing each formation would be one or two cable drum carriers, these being former coaches reduced to their underframes only and equipped with cradles to carry the drums of wire for spooling out.

ABOVE: **Warrington Bank Quay is a hive of activity in October 1972 as Class 25 D5261 stands on the up side of the station in an engineering possession with a very short overhead line maintenance train formed of just two flat-roofed coaches. These are both heavily-rebuilt former LMS vehicles from the DM regional series of departmental coaching stock. Meanwhile, on the left, staff receive instructions as the dismantling of the signal box is in progress.** Simon Bendall Collection

Replacements

It was the London Midland's ex-LMS vehicles that conducted the electrification of the West Coast Main Line, both the original stretch from Euston to Liverpool and Manchester in

Electrifying flat-tops

ABOVE: A closer view of DM395402 at Warrington in October 1972 illustrates many of the key aspects of the overhead line maintenance trains. With the unpowered pantograph raised, staff are assessing the positioning and tensioning of the contact wire from a rather crowded roof-top with a drop of some 14ft to the ground on either side. These half-height coaches were a feature of the DM-series conversions, ladders at the rear of both sections giving access to the roof. Those that survived into the early 1990s tended to have safety railings fitted to the lower half of the coach. *Simon Bendall Collection*

the early 1960s and then the extension on to Glasgow at the beginning of the 1970s. Similarly, it was vehicles of LNER origin that largely maintained the Woodhead route through to its closure in 1981.

It was not until the second half of the 1970s and on into the early 1980s that BR invested heavily in a new fleet of overhead line maintenance (OHLM) trains, these all employing Mk.1 coaches as their conversion fodder. The nature of the rebuilding was largely the same as their predecessors with the same roof, bodyside, and end alterations. One concession to progress was the universal fitting of dual brakes, earlier trains having been vacuum-only.

The formation of these new six-vehicle sets was normally two pantograph-fitted coaches, one at each end, with the remaining types encompassing stores, generator and stores, roof access and stores, and office and staff. In addition to the six still recognisable Mk.1s, at each end was again a cable drum carrier created from a de-bodied sister vehicle, these having strengthened floors to support the cradles.

These new OHLM trains were initially largely deployed along the length of the West Coast Main Line, home depots stretching from Willesden in North London to Glasgow Shields. Some later deliveries additionally went to Romford, Hornsey and Cricklewood (although soon transferred to Bedford) to support the electrified routes out of Liverpool Street, King's Cross and St Pancras, respectively. This influx of new conversions allowed considerable numbers of the older regional vehicles to be withdrawn, particularly of LNER vintage, but many of the ex-LMS types were retained.

Wider use

With the 1980s and early 1990s bringing the expansion of electrification to East Anglia, the East Coast Main Line and around Leeds and Glasgow, the geographical spread of the trains increased considerably. Under the ownership of the Mechanical & Electric Engineers (M&EE) department, two fleets also existed, those allocated to maintenance work with numbers prefixed with an A while those assigned to new electrification projects started with a L, although some mixing occurred. The latter fleet included numerous LMS survivors but also a smaller selection of Mk.1 conversions with home depots during the electrification work including Ipswich, Peterborough, Doncaster Hexthorpe, and Barassie.

As the electrification of the ECML progressed north so too did the coaches with the likes of Heaton, Morpeth and Millerhill serving as centres of operations. Once completed, some of the Mk.1 maintenance sets were redeployed to cover the route with home depots including Portobello (Edinburgh) and Doncaster.

Inevitably, change arrived in the early 1990s as privatisation loomed and the prospect of further widespread electrification looked unlikely. First to be withdrawn were the remaining ex-LMS vehicles while the use of the Mk.1 sets also went into decline as the decade progressed and the new century arrived. This was partly due to the arrival of new track machinery such as trolleys and road/railers equipped with scissor lifts, a process that had begun under BR in the 1980s, but also with increasing health and safety legislation.

A dim view was taken of the risks associated with working on top of the coaches and some efforts were made to improve them. This included trialling a fall arrest system with a harness and safety line connected to a rail along the centreline of the roof while another set received inflatable side skirts, which were impractical as they put the train out of gauge! With the OHLM trains increasingly elderly, requiring the hire of a locomotive to move them and the availability of plant that was faster to deploy, self-propelled and safer to use, the Mk.1 sets were progressively withdrawn in the early 2000s. The last full set was finally sent for scrap in 2010 after five years or so stored at Preston, leaving a few unserviceable stragglers to be dealt with later on.

ABOVE: Making up part of wiring train No.8 on this occasion was workshop coach DM395683, which was converted from LMS Third Open 8341, not that much of the original bodywork is left with the altered doors, windows, and roof. In this pre-TOPS period, just a DM prefix is carried but it would later gain an additional L as part of the new electrification fleet. Its last allocation would be Peterborough with disposal coming in 1995. *Simon Bendall Collection*

ABOVE: Rebuilt in 1960 from another Third Open, workshop and generator coach ADM395615 was still in use 21 years later as it stands in Bedford Yard on August 21, 1981. Behind it is a newly-converted Mk.1 set along with the equally shiny 25kV AC electrification to St Pancras. Proving that the ownership prefix did not always count for much with the M&EE stock, the vehicle was officially allocated to the electrification section so should have carried a LDM prefix, but ADM is applied. It would be scrapped in 1993. *Don Farmborough/Trevor Mann Collection*

Modelling BR Departmental Coaching Stock

Electrifying flat-tops

RIGHT: The overhead line maintenance coaches for the Woodhead route were based at Penistone and were typically of LNER vintage, coming under the Eastern Region's DE series. The Gresley bogies give the origin away of ADE320829 at its home sidings on June 18, 1980, this having been built as non-corridor composite 88147. The electric lights added to the flat roof can be seen along with the bridging plates and high-level jumper cables between the vehicles. This particular coach was fitted out as a workshop vehicle with part of the original door framing visible behind the window mesh. Following the closure of the Pennine route, it was scrapped at Marple & Gillott, Sheffield, in April 1983. *Simon Bendall Collection*

ABOVE: Among the regional series, the office and staff coaches assigned to electrification work were more varied in their look. A condemned LDE320544 lies at Bamfurlong Sidings, Wigan, in April 1982, where it would be scrapped two years later. *Trevor Mann*

ABOVE: Resembling a shed on wheels, ADE320596 was built using a Great Eastern Railway Corridor Composite as its frame. Converted in 1958, it was fitted with a pantograph for contact wire testing and is also seen condemned at Wigan in May 1982. *Trevor Mann*

ABOVE: Built in 1949, LNER Corridor Third 13863 became office coach ADE321131 in 1968. Although lettered for Romford, it is another recorded at Bamfurlong Sidings, Wigan, in September 1982, where it would be scrapped on site five years later. *Trevor Mann*

ABOVE: Converted in 1958, workshop and generator van ADM395334 began life as a Caledonian Railway non-corridor Brake Third. Rebuilt with horizontal planking, it was assigned to the Scottish Region but is seen at Wigan after withdrawal in May 1982. *Trevor Mann*

ABOVE: With the electrified suburban routes out of Liverpool Street and Fenchurch Street, there was a need for stock to be kept in East London. Staff and office coach LDM395709 was stabled at Temple Mills on February 10, 1980. *Simon Bendall Collection*

ABOVE: Not all Electrification department coaches received flat roofs, such as those intended to work with wagons on mast installation trains. Former LMS Corridor Third staff van ADM395409, originally dating from 1924, was again at Wigan in May 1982. *Trevor Mann*

Electrifying flat-tops

ABOVE: The decision to fit the OHLM sets converted from Mk.1s with dual brakes allowed sights such as this to occur. On May 29, 1988, air-braked only 58027 takes a break from its usual merry-go-round coal trains to indulge in a spot of weekend engineering work as it ambles along the relief line at Ampthill, near Bedford. The formation is the standard one for the Mk.1 sets with six coaches sandwiched between the two drum carriers. Martin Loader

RIGHT: From the start of the 1990s, a new livery was introduced for the Mk.1 OHLM sets as they passed through overhaul, this seeing the weather-beaten olive green give way to dark blue with a large red electrification flash symbol. This faded rather badly though as seen at South Kenton on October 19, 1997, as 31255 stands on the up fast line into Euston while some of the staff take a break. The loco was now in EWS ownership with the train also sold to an infrastructure company. Anthony Kay

LEFT: With electrification of the East Coast Main Line underway, 47607 *Royal Worcester* comes off the Royal Border Bridge from the south and into the loop at Berwick-upon-Tweed on August 7, 1988. While the leading cable drum carrier is a former Mk.1, the four coaches are all converted LMS stock. Despite their age, these were still in use as the prestige project required a number of electrification trains and they would continue in service into the early 1990s.
Simon Bendall Collection

Modelling BR Departmental Coaching Stock 31

Electrifying flat-tops

ABOVE: In as-converted condition, QXX pantograph coach ADB975697 was stabled at Wigan Springs Branch, its home depot, on April 27, 1985. Previously a Mk.1 BSK, the lowered pantograph can be glimpsed at the far end while the branding is certainly bold. *Trevor Mann*

ABOVE: Some 11 years later on June 1, 1996, ADB975699 stands in the same position at Springs Branch, this being another pantograph coach rebuilt from a BSK. The early 1990s overhaul programme included the removal of the vacuum brakes, making this a QXA. *Trevor Mann*

ABOVE: Most of the Mk.1 OHLM sets included four different coach types between the two pantograph vehicles, this being the stores coach. ADB975714 was converted from an SK with the yellow fittings on the roof believed to be a trial collapsible safety rope system. *Trevor Mann*

ABOVE: The original olive green livery eventually faded to a grotty grey-green as demonstrated by office and staff coach ADB975741 at Thornaby on June 16, 1996. An ex-SK, this was not a recipient of the blue livery and was scrapped in the summer of 2001. *Mark Saunders*

ABOVE: The slatted sliding door gives ADB975685 away as being a stores and generator coach while doing the job for which it was converted at Mossend on July 22, 1984. The window of the former centre door on what was an SK unusually remains intact. *Trevor Mann*

ABOVE: Another SK had been rebuilt to create stores and roof access coach ADB975734, which is seen at Wigan on June 1, 1996. The roof access was via a wide internal staircase and sliding hatch, the end ladders having covers to prevent unauthorised access. *David Ratcliffe*

ABOVE: Cable drum carrier ADB975905 resides at Springs Branch on April 27, 1985. Notably, only the pantograph coaches had internal handbrakes, having all been converted from brake vehicles, everything else having external handbrake wheels fitted. *Trevor Mann*

ABOVE: The blue livery on the drum carriers was restricted to the lettering panel, the frame otherwise being black and with the white handrails and yellow cradles retained. Once again from the Wigan train, ADB975906 was recorded on June 1, 1996. *David Ratcliffe*

Electrifying flat-tops

ABOVE: Only two of the Mk.1 OHLM sets lasted sufficiently long in traffic to receive the colours of their new privatised owners. On April 5, 2004, Freightliner's 66603 and 66615 top and tail the GTRM-liveried set at Wilson's Crossing., Northampton, while forming the 6Z80 Willesden Brent-Rugby. The smart red and cream livery had been applied to ADB975697/698 and ADB975713/723/733/743 in mid-2002 while the cable drum carriers ADB975898/899 were finished in black. Later based at Bletchley, the whole set was disposed of through Booth's of Rotherham in August 2006. The other repainted set involved ADB975699/700/714/724/734/744 which received mid-blue lower bodies with white above while cable drums ADB975906/907 gained light grey frames. Owned by Carillion, the company's logo was initially carried when outshopped around the start of 2003 but were removed after a few years to leave empty white panels on the blue. Dave Smith

LEFT: Away from the Mk.1-based overhead line stock, the Electrification section also had other modified BR standard coaches on its books. These were fitted out as staff coaches for use with wagon sets, such as the concrete mixing trains, with the main external modification being the fitting of sliding doors at each end and removal of the centre doors. On August 10, 1987. 47367 awaits departure from Clifton Yard, York, with such a formation bound for Doncaster. Behind the Mk.1 and eight bogie bolsters carrying cement mixers are a 22-ton ferry van and Mk.1 BG serving as stores vans. The rear of the train features two Lowmac-mounted auger machines for boring holes for catenary masts, each with an accompanying jib runner, mineral wagon for spoil and brake van. Simon Bendall Collection

RIGHT: A closer look at the Mk.1 staff coach conversions finds LDB975069 at Bedford on August 26, 1980. Converted from SK 24320, the deleted centre door and corridor connection can be seen while the sliding door at the far end is the larger of the two. An external handbrake has also been fitted but unusually this is in the form of a lever rather than a wheel while the weathering effects of working with cement mixers are clear to see. Trevor Mann

Modelling BR Departmental Coaching Stock   33

Electrifying flat-tops

Southern Pride OHLM coaches by Gary Long

The two most interesting coaches in a Mk.1 OHLM train were the pantograph-fitted vehicles at either end, which tested the contact wire once work was completed. This is the Southern Pride etched kit finished as ADB975708 from the Bletchley set.

When installing the overhead wires for electrification, the workers used to walk along the roof of the flat-topped coaches. Imagine doing this in all weathers while the train was moving, with no guardrails and 95mph trains passing on adjacent lines. Two good videos exist on YouTube showing the operation of the trains, entitled British Rail Electrification 1/2 and 2/2, the second part being the more enlightening.

I have modelled a shortened electrification train using the Southern Pride Models etched brass kits, this featuring three coaches and two cable drum wagons, which is the maximum length I can fit on my layout. The former Mk.1s encompass a pantograph coach, generator vehicle and staff coach and were not chosen to match any specific set but to provide a selection of the most obvious vehicles that would be required.

I was impressed with the contents, given this was the first time I had built a model from a kit. The body of the coaches is comprised of brass sides, roof, and end panels, while there is a further separate roof section that is also formed of brass. The chassis is plastic and requires the detail parts to be added along with Bachman bogies, which give good running characteristics, but the train is certainly a heavy one.

The instructions consist of a page of double-sided A4 text and a couple of additional hand-drawn sketches. If you follow the instructions and study the diagrams, it is obvious how the kits go together, and I had no issues with assembly.

Body assembly
The main coach sides are supplied pre-shaped but strangely the additional roof section comes flat and needs the edges folded over by around 3mm. I tried a few methods for folding this but in the end, I acquired a set of folding bars. This is my only quibble with the kit, given the sides are supplied already shaped. I originally purchased only one coach but when building the other pair, it was just as quick to build two at a time and would recommend this to anyone considering building more than one of the kits.

Due to the size of the materials being soldered together, you need a fair bit of heat, and I used a 40 watt soldering iron supplemented with a kitchen blowtorch, as necessary. I used resin-cored solder but also a decent quality flux. A set of leather gardening gloves are also useful when holding pieces together or adjusting parts while soldering. The ends of the coaches were a little tricky to get right but by persevering, they can be soldered together.

The mesh window grilles and the rectangular frames on the roof for the lights were then soldered onto the body, although they can be glued if preferred. There are small marks on the roof to show where the lights need to be located and I used wooden lollipop sticks to hold the items in place while the solder cooled. At this stage, I also fixed the whitemetal door frames in place using epoxy glue and opened up the holes for the handrails using a small handheld drill.

Detail additions
On the chassis, various parts are supplied to add to the frame moulding, these including V-hangers, air brake parts and solebar lights among others, all made from a mix of materials including brass, plastic, whitemetal and resin printed. Additional pipework was also added using brass rod.

I used Railmatch Network SouthEast dark blue as the main colour with the shoulders of the roof finished with white enamel and the central walkways in grey. Southern Pride supplies the waterslide transfers separately, each sheet being sufficient for one coach with a few spares. Also offered is a sheet of pre-cut white vinyl labels to represent the glass of the solebar lights, these being applied over the top of the whitemetal light castings.

With the transfers in place, the glazing was then added, which was cut from clear flat sheet. As the coach sides are so thin, this was simply stuck to the inside of the body with the mesh window grilles partially obscuring the glazing. Roof conduit was then added using brass rod that had been sprayed orange in advance and the plastic roof lights glued into their frames and painted.

Drum carriers
Unlike the coaches, the cable drum carriers are largely brass in their construction with the plastic underframe trusses being affixed

ABOVE: With the body assembled and window grilles in place, the coaches can be given an undercoat before any of the finer details are added, this also highlights any imperfections.

ABOVE: With the painting completed and transfers in place, work to fit the roof lights and conduit is in progress. Some touching up of the roof grey will be necessary afterwards.

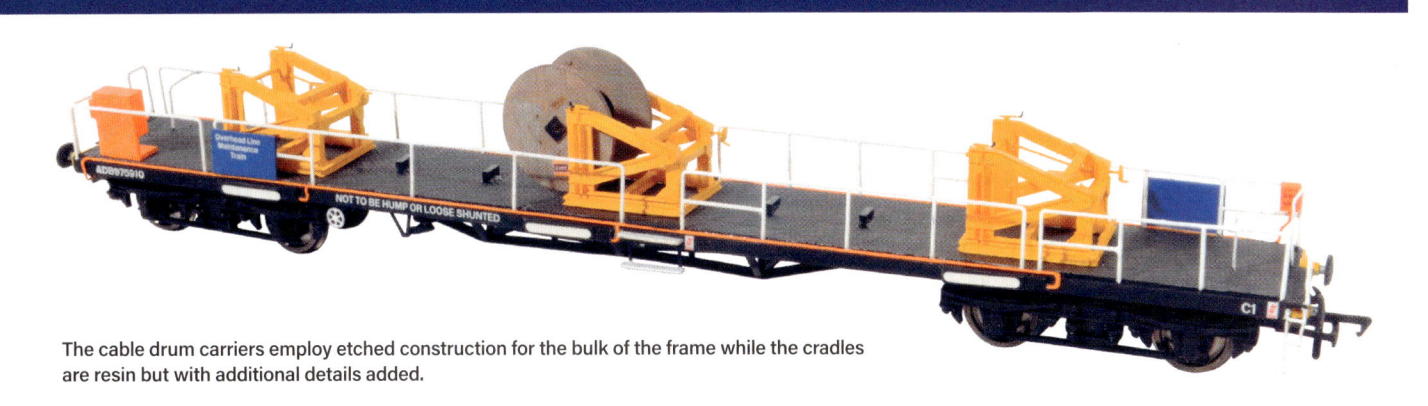

Electrifying flat-tops

The cable drum carriers employ etched construction for the bulk of the frame while the cradles are resin but with additional details added.

RIGHT: A view of the underside of a drum carrier shows the bogie mounting and some of the detailing while the MDF pieces used to protect the handrails are also in place.

to a flat piece of plastic which is then glued to the underside of the chassis. Similarly, the bogies are each connected to a whitemetal casting via a brass bolt with the complete assemblies then glued to the chassis using epoxy glue.

Once the handrails were soldered in position, they were found to be delicate and easily bent. To avoid further damage, I made some packing pieces from MDF and positioned these behind the handrails, making the models much easier to handle. For the deck, there is a section of plastic sheet with a chequer plate effect moulded on. This can be glued in place once everything else is soldered in place, including the handrails. The cradles are supplied with the kit and are resin mouldings, these receiving a little extra detail to enhance them. In contrast, the actual cable drums are available separately from Southern Pride.

RIGHT: Given the absence of decent quality 4mm scale pantographs, I used an HO scale model of a Stone-Faiveley type as produced by Sommerfeldt. The base size was a little narrow for the larger scale, so I cut off the original legs and soldered on new ones made from 0.65mm square brass bent to fit and with the insulators fitted over the top of the vertical sections. To the right, the roller on which the wires run when being installed was fabricated from pieces of plastic and glued onto the roof after painting.

Another of the completed Mk.1 OHLM coaches, this being the generator vehicle as evidenced by the bodyside slats.

Modelling BR Departmental Coaching Stock   35

A home from home

The need to transport staff to worksites was one of the initial reasons for creating departmental coaching stock. This practice became more specialised as infrastructure work increasingly turned to mechanisation with operators of cranes and ballast machines needing to travel with their equipment and have amenities close by, as Simon Bendall details.

The category of staff vehicles is certainly one of the broadest to be found in the field of departmental stock. Different railways and then regions had varying ideas of what staff would put up with, some opting for converted wooden-planked vans while others went for the more luxurious option of adapted coaching stock, be it four-axle, six-axle, or bogie designs.

Modifying surplus brake vans was a popular option as they already had a stove installed for heating and the presence of a handbrake was always useful. Unwanted verandah areas could also be rebuilt without much difficultly to increase the living space, as was common on the ex-GWR Toads. Under BR, half-brake coaches offered a brake area that could be fitted out as a mess space while the passenger compartments lent themselves to conversion into dormitories. Perhaps surprisingly, sleeper coaches were not common in such a role under BR, the Scottish Region having a small number of ex-LMS and Mk.1s as full dormitory coaches that largely failed to make the 1980s while the use of Mk.3s was ever rarer.

The Civil Engineers department was undoubtedly the biggest user of staff coaches, be they with or without dormitory facilities, in both the BR and regional number series. The Signal and Telegraph Engineers were also well covered but the Mechanical and Electrical Engineers had far less general stock. There was of course those already seen in the department's breakdown trains and OHLM sets but the other main group was those based on the Southern Region with the Power Supply Section.

As already mentioned, staff coaches and vans were another category that suffered heavily as health and safety legislation took effect in the 1990s, the appearance of new external gas heating ventilators, fire exit signage and even the fitting of fire suppression systems in a handful of cases all indicating the areas that were problematic. Large scale withdrawals were the result in the first half of the decade with many vehicles passing into preservation. As the following pages show, the few that were able to continue in use only made it to the mid-2000s with engineers' staff coaches now long gone from the network.

ABOVE: Time was running out for staff coach DB975220 as it rolls through Newport on February 15, 1995, behind Mainline Freight-owned 37046 on an eastbound engineers' working. The coach had been repainted in chocolate and cream in late 1992 and served around Exeter and the West Country for a number of years. It was scrapped in October 1996. Two more departmental coaches are also on view, the most obvious being Satlink red/yellow-liveried KDB977591 in the background, which was a long-term static resident of Godfrey Road stabling point. The other is DB975414, the match wagon to RM62 ballast cleaner DR76218, which was built on a Mk.1 BSK underframe so still classified as coaching stock. Making up the rest of the train are three YCV Turbots. *Simon Bendall Collection*

RIGHT: Rebuilt from a Maunsell-design Second Open, ADS70196 was a M&EE staff and tool coach that was converted in 1963 and initially based at Hither Green. On April 5, 1980, it was to be found at Guildford and some 16 months from withdrawal, scrapping coming at the end of 1981. The olive green livery and minimal branding was common for the department's Southern-based stock. *Simon Bendall Collection*

A home from home

Southern staff vans

The Southern Region made considerable use of the various types of four-wheel non-passenger vans built by its predecessor, the wooden bodywork lending itself to easy conversion into staff vehicles, these often serving as tool vans as well or sometimes with a dormitory role. A good number survived in traffic into the early 1990s and could be found well beyond Southern territory by this time.

RIGHT: **Of all the Southern types, it was the Parcels and Miscellaneous Vans (PMV) that were preferred for departmental use with large numbers transferred across. Seen at Woking on August 25, 1980, DS146 was entirely typical of the staff and tool vans converted for Civil Engineers use. A near universal alteration was the addition of a window in each end beneath the ventilator while a through air pipe has also been added, giving a QPW TOPS code. Built in 1936, this evenly-planked example would be scrapped in 1989.** Simon Bendall Collection

ABOVE: **In contrast, the Southern-design Covered Carriage Trucks (CCT) were less numerous as staff and tool vans, quite possibly because of the extra work required to seal the end doors. Also recorded at Woking on August 25, 1980, DS70243 shows the different treatment of the ends with the additional window offset and replacing a vent. Metal strapping has been used to seal the doors at the far end with the locking mechanism also removed, while other CCTs also had the remaining vents plated over.** Simon Bendall Collection

ABOVE: **Continuing the donor trend, the Southern passenger guard's vans (BY) were quite rare in departmental use. With three extra windows cut into the ends, ADB975143 was a staff and tool van for the M&EE's Power Supply Section when recorded at Horsham on July 31, 1979. The West Sussex yard was the home of the PSS fleet and housed a diverse collection of stock into the 1990s. This van later passed to Signal and Telegraph use and survives at the Bluebell Railway.** Simon Bendall Collection

ABOVE: **Converted in 1978 from a plywood-bodied PMV, Civil Engineers staff and dormitory van DB975962 shows a number of differences to DS146 at Newport Alexandra Dock Junction on April 20, 1984. The end window is larger and the ventilator above removed while vents for the gas heating have been added to the bodysides and an additional window cut into the far door. The van has not received a through air pipe though while the nearer door is lettered 'Emergency Fire Door'.** Trevor Mann

ABOVE: **Also a former PMV, Civil Engineers staff and tool van DB975669 shows further changes at Tonbridge West Yard on April 21, 1991. The right-hand hinged wooden doors have been completely replaced by an inward opening door with consequential changes to the surrounding bodywork and window. The other set of doors is sealed shut with a heating vent added, the underframe box below containing the gas bottles. It is also now air-braked and vacuum-piped as a QPB.** Simon Bendall Collection

A home from home

Southern staff vans in 4mm by Paul Wade

DS70249
This staff and tool van was a former CCT used with Plasser and Theurer ballast cleaner DR76214 and then viaduct inspection unit DR82100. This was coded QPW, denoting a vacuum-braked van with a thorough air pipe. The main construction began by fixing one end to one side and then repeating for the other side, before joining the two sections together to form the basic body. The roof was fitted only once the body had been fixed to the chassis and painting and glazing were finished.

However, before making the body, the sides and ends required alterations to reflect the van's departmental use.

Although originally a CCT, it was easier to use the Parkside PMV kit as the basis for this model as DS70249 had lost its end doors in favour of plain panelling and strengthening ribs. The plank detail was therefore sanded off the ends and the top vent cut off, leaving the vertical ribs behind. On the bodysides, the four waist-height vents were not fitted as these had been plated over on the real van with the plates represented using five-thou styrene rectangles. The earlier iteration of the Parkside kit has these side vents moulded on, making removal much more difficult, so something to keep in mind when sourcing a kit. The doors were also modified as described elsewhere on this page.

The underframe had two gas bottle holders added, one on each side and made from 20-thou plastic sheet and strip. A vacuum cylinder was fitted at one end while, on the roof, the rain strips were modified to the appropriate straight profile using 28mm long plastic strips. The moulded curved rain strips were carved off with two torpedo vents added, one at each end.

The grey/yellow 'Dutch' livery employed Phoenix Precision faded signal yellow and Railfreight grey, the latter also including the solebars and ends. Transfers were mostly individual letters and numbers with some items from various wagon sheets for maintenance boxes and overhead warning signs.

DS1385
This older QPW staff and tool van was an ex-PMV used with Plasser & Theurer twin jib crane DRP78224; a Parkside PMV kit with even plank spacing again being used as the starting point. Like other Southern staff vans that lasted into the early 1990s, several modifications were made late in this van's life that do not apply to earlier periods so, as ever, photos from your chosen period should be consulted.

One of the most obvious alterations was to the original sets of double doors. At one end on both sides, these were completely removed and replaced with a larger single door that opened inwards, providing extra safety, although which side the hinges were on varied between vehicles. As this new door was not as wide as the previous double doors, an additional section of bodywork was added to fill the gap.

This new door area was formed by filing off the moulded doors and then cutting the new window into the plastic, ensuring it had rounded corners. Microstrip was then added vertically to form the door frame followed by the door handle, made from a small section of strip, and two wire handrails after painting.

In contrast, the end windows found in many Southern staff vans were a much older modification and typically dated from their initial conversion to provide extra light into otherwise dingy interiors. The size and shape varied but once the hole is made, it can be framed with 10-thou by 30-thou Microstrip. The chassis again received gas bottle lockers and a vacuum cylinder with new 21mm rain strips on the roof but no vents. The all-over yellow again employed faded signal yellow with lettering formed from individual characters.

DB975669

Another former PMV, this was a staff and tool van for ballast cleaner DR76317 but notable as having been converted to air brakes with a through vacuum pipe, making it a QPB. The Parkside kit was again the basis but this time one with the alternating wide and narrow bodyside planking.

When vans received the new door at one end on both sides, the original double doors at the other end were invariably sealed shut but only on one side, this leaving the opposing pair as an emergency exit. This modification was obvious as a metal strip was added down the centre of the doors. This was recreated by sanding flat the joint between the doors to remove the handles and other details with a strip of five-thou plastic then added vertically in three pieces and positioned in between the elongated strap hinges.

This door usually had a gas vent for one of the heaters added as well, which can be made from a square of five-thou plastic with a round section of 2mm diameter rod and a 10-thou strip on the top positioned at an angle. The gas bottle cabinets were added as before, but the brake equipment this time was a 12mm air cylinder and accompanying distributor. The paint was Phoenix Precision's olive green with weathering applied over the top to dull it down.

DS70242

This QPW staff and tool van was an ex-CCT assigned to twin jib crane DRS78210, the model using the vintage Wrenn RTR model, this having uneven planking. This example also retained its end doors with three of the ventilators staying in place but the fourth converted into an offset end window. Although larger than the PMV version, the windows were made in the same way as described for DS1385.

On the side with the retained set of double doors, one of the centre windows was plated over with 20-thou plastic sheet in the opening and finished with a five-thou cover plate over the top. On this example, both gas bottle cabinets were found on the same side with the bufferbeams receiving both air and vacuum pipes. A mix of browns was used to represent the typical filthy condition these vans got into with further weathering added using watercolours. Finally, the glazing was painted with matt varnish to represent dirty windows.

ADB975424

This staff and tool van was a former PMV used by the M&EE Power Supply Section. This was coded QPV with an evenly-planked Parkside PMV again the origin. This van had the fewest modifications with just the sealed door on one side and a window in only one end. It also had a stove pipe on the roof at one end, this being made from 1mm plastic pipe on a small five-thou plastic base, along with two torpedo vents. On the underframe, extra brake rods and safety loops were fitted while the livery was again a brown mix. The late Barrie Swann made this particular model.

A home from home

Western staff coaches

The Western Region seemingly had a higher regard for their staff's comfort than the Southern as the majority of its staff vehicle conversions in the regional DW series employed ex Great Western coaches, it preferring to leave draughty, wooden-planked vans for the transport of tools and stores. However, this did change somewhat once conversions into the British Rail DB series commenced.

RIGHT: Some of the last conversions in the DW number series around 1967 were a batch of 18 Hawksworth-design Brake Third Corridor coaches, which all became staff and dormitory vehicles for the Civil Engineers. Many of these were partnered with on-track plant, such as DW150392 which was recorded at Radyr Yard on April 5, 1983, accompanying RM74 ballast cleaner DR76308. Some of these lasted into the early 1990s, allowing them to be snapped up by preserved lines, this one finding salvation at Didcot Railway Centre. *Trevor Mann*

ABOVE: Another of the Hawksworth staff and dormitory coaches is seen at Ellesmere Port on August 13, 1983, the paintwork of DW150400 being rather tatty compared to its sister vehicle. This was in use with single line track-relaying gantries, these collapsible machines being carried on top of Lowmac well wagons when not in use. Although the coach was lettered to work with the Secmafer-built M9 design, this had not been updated and it was actually paired with two newer Donelli PD350 machines. *Trevor Mann*

ABOVE: Built at Swindon Works in 1933, Collett-design Corridor Brake Third 5786 was converted into Civil Engineers staff and dormitory coach DW150338 in 1962. Some 19 years later, it could be found accompanying a Plasser and Theurer RM62 ballast cleaner at Longport on April 17, 1981, the white stripes being applied only on this end of the blue livery. Last based at Crewe Gresty Road, it was in use until early 1993 but was broken up at Willesden soon afterwards. *Trevor Mann*

ABOVE: Some GWR design wooden-bodied non-passenger stock did find its way into departmental use as staff vans, these being something of a step down to modified Hawksworth or Collett coaches. A well-known example is Fruit D van DB975411, which was built by BR after nationalisation, and became a staff and dormitory van for a Plasser and Theurer GPC-72 telescopic jib engineers' crane. This included window and door alterations that were later reversed after passing into preservation. *Paul Bartlett*

ABOVE: British Railways built further Fruit D vans between 1956-60, these receiving BR numbers rather than using the GWR series. Originally 92061, this became staff and dormitory van DB975336 for the Civil Engineers and was recorded at Bristol East Depot on April 12, 1985. The conversion is notably different to its sister with both outer doors modified, a heater vent installed, and a compartment created for the storage of spare gas cylinders. These alterations remain in place today at Peak Rail. *Trevor Mann*

A home from home

Modelling a Hawksworth staff coach by Greg Brookes

When Hornby brought out its range of Hawksworth coaching stock in 4mm scale, there was an opportunity to use these as a basis for some engineering conversions. The Brake Third Corridor was a suitable starting point for Civil Engineers staff and dormitory coach DW150401, which was selected as I had good photos available of both sides to ensure everything would be accurate. These were taken by my friend Paul James and are viewable on his Jamerail Flickr site www.flickr.com/photos/95430950@N07. Pictures of the same coach are also on Paul Bartlett's web site.

The prototype was originally a Hawksworth-designed BTK to diagram 133 and numbered 2233. This batch of coaches was completed in November 1950 by the Birmingham Railway Carriage and Wagon Company and were the last coaches to have been ordered by the Great Western Railway, albeit built after nationalisation. The last Hawksworth corridor coaches were all withdrawn from service at the end of December 1967 and 18 BTKs were then converted for departmental use, being numbered DW150390-407. DW150401 was paired with DRP78219, a twin-jib track re-layer working at one time out of Newport.

Modifications

The conversion uses a Hornby BTK as its basis, the first stage being to dismantle the coach and remove and plate over the gangway connections. Various doors and windows were also plated over to match the photos. Two of the windows appeared to have hardboard fitted internally which was represented with suitably coloured masking tape applied from the inside.

Additional roof filler pipes were added to the brake end while handrails and footsteps were put in place by the central door on one side and by the saloon end door on the other. On the underframe, external handbrake levers and V hangers were required on both sides, these coming from the spares box. The solebar footboards were pared back to just be under the two remaining doors and an external vacuum pipe running down one side of the solebar was replicated with plastic rod.

The most difficult part of the conversion was sourcing and fitting the individual heating vents with there being four on one side and two on the other. These were initially omitted until it became possible to produce bespoke 3D-printed parts, which were designed and printed by my friend Jonny Duffett. These heating vents were seen on many staff vehicle conversions and the files for these are now available as free downloads from www.thingiverse.com/ironmink/designs should you wish to use them on your own projects.

The coach was re-gauged to EM gauge to run on Shenston Road and Accurascale screw couplings were fitted. I run it paired with a heavily altered Airfix kit for the Booth Rodley diesel hydraulic cranes, which has received a scratchbuilt chassis and match wagon. Finally, the model was repainted in engineer's olive drab from the Railmatch range, while the transfers were assembled from various bits and pieces. It was then weathered to match the images I had available.

A home from home

Eastern staff coaches

The Eastern Region favoured using actual coaches to carry personnel around, be they LNER vehicles of both Gresley and Thompson origin or earlier constituent designs. Riding on Gresley bogies, they were perhaps some of the best staff coaches available, even if those wooden-panelled vehicles that received engineer's green with yellow doors looked somewhat incongruous.

RIGHT: Even by departmental coaching stock standards, DE320444 was particularly vintage, having been built as part of the East Coast Joint Stock fleet in 1907. Originally a Corridor Third, it was now serving as a staff and dormitory coach for Plasser & Theurer track-relayer DRP78218 and assigned to work across the Eastern Region. Seen in September 1981 at an unidentified location, it is now owned by the LNER Coach Association. To the left, 12-ton van DB767786 was also allocated to the crane as a tool van. Simon Bendall Collection

ABOVE: Converted from a short-framed LNER non-corridor Third, DE3280803 was a staff and tool van for the Civil Engineers. Initially built in 1927 by the Gloucester Railway Carriage and Wagon Company, it was repurposed in 1960 and was recorded awaiting disposal at Lowestoft 26 years later on August 12, 1986. Lettered 'Mess & Tool Van Ipswich' and with a QPV TOPS code, it would be sold the following year to the Mangapps Railway Museum, where it still resides. Trevor Mann

ABOVE: Altogether more modern was DE321134, a Civil Engineers staff and dormitory coach converted from a Thompson-design Corridor Brake Third. Built in 1950, the former 16868 had less than two decades of passenger use before being re-tasked as a support coach to ballast cleaner DR76105. On May 29, 1984, it was stabled at York Leeman Road and displaying the common lettering stating it was not to be uncoupled from its accompanying track machine. Trevor Mann

ABOVE: Back when departmental coaches resided at far flung outposts of the network, Perth division-allocated DE321056 was to be found at Wick on September 21, 1978. Of Gresley origin, the Civil Engineers staff and dormitory coach dated from 1938 as a Corridor Composite. All but one of the doors had been sealed and an external handbrake added among other modifications. It would remain in BR stock for another decade until broken up on site at Inverkeithing in 1988. Simon Bendall Collection

ABOVE: Built back in 1936 as a Third Corridor. DE320946 had remarkably just emerged from a full overhaul when stabled at Peterborough Spital Sidings on March 12, 1990. Another Civil Engineers staff and dormitory coach, it seemingly saw little further use and was sold to members of the LNER Coach Association a decade later. One wonders what Gresley would have made of one of his coaches adorned with heating vents, wasp stripes and an orange cantrail line! Simon Bendall Collection

A home from home

Midland staff coaches

Coming to the last of the regional profiles, the London Midland Region was also in favour of re-using coaches for staff transport with considerable numbers of ex-LMS vehicles being repurposed. It was not above using the odd wooden-bodied van though such as for the mobile workshops used by Pooley & Son Ltd for maintaining weighing equipment across the region.

RIGHT: A fine view of DM395778 at Warrington in October 1972, which was built for the LMS in 1928 as a convertible sleeper. This was a Signal and Telegraph Engineers staff and dormitory coach, the supplementary lettering stating 'Electrification, to be returned to Brook Sidings, Crewe' and would have been in the area due to the re-signalling that was ongoing around Warrington at this time. It survives today, albeit in need of restoration, at the Midland Railway - Butterley. *Simon Bendall Collection*

ABOVE: Despite its all-red livery, DM395828 was not a breakdown crane coach but rather allocated to Watford Junction as an area Civil Engineers staff and tool coach. Converted in 1963, it had begun life 30 years earlier as an LMS Period III Third Corridor. As can be seen through the windows, the compartment interior had been completely stripped out for an open plan arrangement. Recorded at home on May 10, 1980, it was scrapped at Marple & Gillott in January 1985. *Simon Bendall Collection*

ABOVE: Another Civil Engineers staff and tool coach eschewing a traditional look at Watford Junction was DM395895 on August 2, 1980. Using an LMS Period III BTK dating from 1935 as its basis, its departmental career had commenced in 1964 but was over by the mid-1980s with storage at Northampton and then Bescot. Sold to the East Lancashire Railway in the early 1990s, the body was soon scrapped, leaving the chassis to serve as a materials carrier until cut in 2009. *Simon Bendall Collection*

ABOVE: Originally an LMS Period I Corridor Composite, DM395816 was already 50 years old when captured residing at Warrington Arpley on August 7, 1980. At this time, it was serving as a staff and dormitory coach for track relayer DRS78206, which can just be seen to the left, and could be found working anywhere on the London Midland Region. It would be partnered with a modern Cowans track relayer later in the decade, but it was in store by 1987 and would be scrapped in 1989. *Simon Bendall Collection*

ABOVE: Another staff and dormitory coach that could wander widely was DM395912, which was allocated to work with track relayer DRB78121. Converted in 1965, this was originally a Period III non-corridor Third built in 1937. On September 18, 1982, and six years from disposal. it was stabled among the cement Presflos at Earles Sidings awaiting its next duty. As was typically the case with staff coaches, the number of doors still in use was much reduced, just one out of eight in this case. *Trevor Mann*

Modelling BR Departmental Coaching Stock 43

A home from home

On the pleasant summer's day of August 4, 1988, BR blue 47463 ambles along the down slow at Waltham St Lawrence, between Maidenhead and Reading, with a Civil Engineers working. Leading the formation is a Plasser and Theurer TJC-60 track relayer, often known as a twin jib crane, with an accompanying Mk.1 staff coach, this being a former BSK. The rest of the visible portion features six YCV Turbot ballast opens and at least ten ZFV Dogfish ballast hoppers. *Simon Bendall Collection*

British Rail staff coaches

With British Rail's DB series of departmental coaching stock containing the best part of 2,000 vehicles, it is fair to say the fleet of staff, tool and dormitory coaches was diverse and picturing them all is impossible. This selection is therefore focussed on those in use with the Civil Engineers as these are perhaps the most useful to modellers seeking to bring interest to their ballast trains. The coaches of other operations, such as Satlink and Project Mercury, have been covered to a degree in previous volumes in this series, while further staff coaches with specialised allocations appear in the following chapters.

ABOVE: In unrelieved olive green, DB975535 was a staff, tool and dormitory coach assigned to the Soil Mechanics Section of the Civil Engineers. Converted around 1970, it is seen a decade later at South Lambeth freight depot on August 23, 1980. Notionally based at Wimbledon Engineers' Yard at this time, it could travel countrywide when required. Converted from a Mk.1 BSK, various doors, windows and the corridor connections have been removed while the handbrake is now external with a centrally-positioned lever. By the end of the decade, it had been reassigned as a staff coach for tunnel inspection trains. *Trevor Mann*

ABOVE: An early Mk.1 staff and dormitory conversion in 1972, former BCK DB975199 displays a number of alterations at York Leeman Road on May 29, 1984. Its lettering variously reads 'Messing and living van', 'Return to Leeman Road York', and 'CCE Dept E. Region, to travel with ballast cleaner 76305'. Notably the latter number was newer, having replaced the previous machine DR76212. Two gas bottle lockers have been added to the underframe while a trait of Eastern Region Civil Engineers coaches was to paint the functional doors yellow to brighten up the olive green. *Trevor Mann*

A home from home

ABOVE: Staff and dormitory coach DB975379 is still recognisable as a former SK, the external alterations on this side being limited to a heating vent, removed gangways and gas bottle lockers. However, the other side had five recessed vents and the centre door removed. Seen in Dringhouses Yard, York, on April 24, 1983, the coach began the decade as part of the Eastern Region's weedkiller set but ended it as a companion for ballast cleaners. Trevor Mann

ABOVE: QPV DB975538 was an experiment to provide a new fleet of staff and dormitory vehicles for the Civil Engineers by mounting two Portacabins on a Mk.1 underframe. Assigned to the London Midland, it was partnered with track relayer DRB78113 for evaluation and is seen at Chester in July 1986. However, it did not find favour as it was too hot in the summer and too cold in the winter! Out of use by 1992, it was scrapped at Booth's Rotherham yard four years later. David Ratcliffe

ABOVE: Another unusual staff and dormitory van was DE321107, which was initially rebuilt from a Mk.1 horsebox into an inspection saloon in 1966, complete with end windows and finished in olive green. As the conversion took place before the introduction of the DB number series in 1970, it went into the Eastern's DE series, one of only a handful of Mk.1s to gain a regional number. The 1970s saw it become a staff van and for a time it worked with a Lowmac converted into a gauging vehicle. By May 29, 1984, this role had ceased when stabled at York Leeman Road. Disposal would come in 1995 at MC Metals, Glasgow. Trevor Mann

ABOVE: A number of Mk.1 CCTs found use as staff and dormitory coaches, some receiving quite extensive alterations to their sides and ends. ADB977019 was not one of these but had still gained a heating vent, small grille, tweaks to the doors, through air pipe, underframe steps and gas cylinder lockers along with Civil Engineers grey/yellow. A Western-based van, it was lettered 'To work with ABC (sic) 76308', 'BC' being a common abbreviation for ballast cleaner. It is seen at the Battlefield Line on August 31, 1998, after withdrawal but would be scrapped in 2009 following a stint at Ruddington. Simon Bendall Collection

ABOVE: When first converted in 1970, DB975017 was a welding instruction coach before being repurposed a decade or so later as a staff and dormitory coach, again to work with a ballast cleaner throughout the Western Region. Originally a Mk.1 BSO, the common removal of some doors and windows has taken place along with the gangway connections. Underframe alterations included extra steps, an external handbrake wheel and gas cylinder storage but it remained resolutely vacuum brake-only as a QXV. Seen at Radyr on April 28, 1991, scrapping came five years later. Hywel Thomas

ABOVE: Former Mk.1 bullion van 99202 was a late addition to the Civil Engineers staff coach fleet in 1990, becoming QPX DB977692 and, inevitably, the support vehicle for a Western Region ballast cleaner. However, when recorded at Newport Alexandra Dock Junction on September 23 the same year, it had yet to start this role and was accompanying some Donelli track-relayers. Sold into preservation in the mid-1990s, it was initially housed at the Gloucestershire-Warwickshire Railway but is now located at the Strathspey. Hywel Thomas

A home from home

Support stock for a ballast cleaner by Mark Lambert

Little and large! These two support vehicles from an Eastern Region ballast cleaner turned up on loan in the consist of a single-line relaying train on the Southern in 1986, this being in connection with the electrification of the Hastings line. The Mk.1 coach is a simple renumbering of a Hornby model, the manufacturer having produced three similar releases in olive green a year or so ago, just with different numbers and lettering.

The donor saw all of the markings, apart from the number, removed with high-grade (2500-3000 grit) nail-polishers and then one digit changed at the end of the number to become DB975803. I removed the battery boxes and the regulator frame and replaced them with Southern Pride gas bottle cabinets in the correct locations. The underframe then received a coat of Army Painter 'Hardened Carapace' to cover up the butchery.

The 12-ton van is a Parkside kit (PC42) for the BR fruit vans and is built straight from the packet with some additional brake gear detailing, such as yokes, rigging and safety loops, and then finished in faded bauxite. I mixed some Games Workshop paints to give a good shade for the 1980s condition of this van and then dry-brushed a dark brown colour over the top to give a patchy finish, especially on the plywood sides. Small areas were next painted with fresh bauxite to match the real van's touch-ups and I used light and dark brown acrylic washes to simulate staining and rust. These were applied over a number of days until I was happy with the effect and the final colour.

I reproduced the working instructions panel using individual letters laid onto the model. These were Railtec one-inch and two-inch scale letters placed with the aid of a magnifying glass over a couple of sessions. The TOPS code, weight, DB875120 number and tare weight are laid out rather oddly. As far as I can tell, the number is in its original location and everything else has been fitted round it. One of the maintenance panels is also laid out unusually in order to fit in with the strapping on the side.

Most of these transfers were Railtec items, although the number came from the pack supplied with the model with the digits suitably rearranged. I have since found out that the roof profile on this kit is slightly wrong and that the sides (but not the ends) should be extended in height by about 1mm to flatten the roof profile out a bit. A modification for another day perhaps.

ABOVE: Eastern Region ballast cleaners invariably ran with a supporting staff coach and tool van as seen at Cambridge on April 15, 1988. Departing from the station sidings to the south, 31196 has a RM74 machine in tow along with a Mk.1 staff coach and a Vanwide as the tool van. The leading wagon is a SPA taken into departmental stock as a ZAA Pike and seemingly loaded with scrap point rodding from the ongoing modernisation and electrification of the area. A BR brake van is also visible on the rear due to brake incompatibility. Simon Bendall Collection

A regional staff coach for Tonbridge by Paul Wade

ABOVE: The olive green side of DS70247 showing the former passenger end detail, mid-bodyside gas vent and the standard layout of lettering for a Southern-based Civil Engineers coach.

A quirk of the regional numbering system for departmental coaches was that a conversion went into the number series of the region conducting the work rather than the one from where the coach originated. Thus, when LMS Period III Brake Composite Corridor 6815 was turned into a staff and dormitory coach by the Southern Region in 1967, it was numbered DS70247 rather than taking a number in the Midland's DM series. This was then assigned to work with a Plasser & Theurer ballast cleaner for much of its life.

Built in 4mm scale to run on Tonbridge West Yard, the basis was a Phoenix aluminium kit. Once the sides were cleaned up, there was one change to the window layout to be carried out, this seeing a single main pane plated over on one side with a gas vent fitted at the bottom. This was achieved with 20-thou styrene sheet cut to a good fit and with the opening for the vent filed out. A further two vents were also needed, centrally-positioned on each bodyside, so these were also cut out of the sides as the next step.

The sides were glued to the ends with epoxy adhesive after ensuring that the cast ends fitted nicely with the aluminium sides. Before fitting the roof, this required the holes drilling out for the vents while roof ribs were also added using Microstrip lengths curved by running them through your fingers and glued on with liquid polystyrene cement. The guard's van end was plain in appearance with just two lamp brackets made from staples. The other end had two lamp brackets along with water fillers and brake butterfly valves, the latter items being made from 0.5mm wire and Microstrip sections. The door and luggage van vents were not fitted to the sides as they had been removed on this coach.

Underframe assembly

The first task was to fit the separate solebars to the floor, after which stepboards were added in the appropriate positions beneath the doors, these again being made from Microstrip. Then came the cast buffers while the gas bottle cabinets on the underframe were fabricated from 20-thou styrene sheet and strip. Whitemetal handbrake levers and vacuum cylinders were next sourced from a rummage in the spares box.

The bogies were Bachmann's LMS type bolted onto the chassis with rivet washers used to obtain the correct ride height. The floor was fixed to the inner ends of the body by drilling and tapping for 10BA bolts. Other touches included adding a mix of shell and torpedo cast roof vents while the top fitting of the water filler pipes was a slice of a 2mm round sprue. The guard's doors had their handrails added with brass handles and grabs on the other doors as needed.

The body was painted in Humbrol green (No.76) on one side along with the solebar and underframe trussing. However, the other side, solebar and both ends were finished in olive green; I think the sides were different colours due to a partial repaint after a graffiti attack. The door edges and hinges were drawn on with a black edding pen with the rest of the chassis in brown.

The transfers were mostly separate letters and numbers and much more basic on the repainted green side where only a crude number was re-applied. Finally, most of the glazing was painted with matt varnish on the inside to represent the dirty look of the windows, while the toilet window and those either side of it were painted brown on the inside to match the reference photos.

ABOVE: The mid-green side of the former LMS BCK shows the plated-over window and the extra vent found on this side. The partial green repaint not only included the solebar but also the trussing, while the lettering was limited to a number and DS prefix that were not only different sizes but also different colours!

A home from home

Balfour Beatty coaches

Of all the infrastructure maintenance companies that emerged from the early years of privatisation, it was Balfour Beatty that invested the most in staff coaches. These came from two sources, firstly in 1998 when it purchased the three Mk.1 support coaches from the Nomix-Chipman weedkilling train. This set had become redundant at the end of the previous year and while Railtrack acquired the actual spray coach, this left CC99016-18 available for sale.

Moved to Balfour Beatty's Ashford depot, all three received the company's white and blue livery but their subsequent use in traffic appears to have been limited. A handful of photos show the odd example formed in infrastructure trains working off Hoo Junction around 2000 and always accompanying one or two of Balfour's ex-BR Plasser and Theurer GPC-72 cranes. However, much of their time seems to have been spent stabled at Ashford and the trio were sold into preservation or further non-railway use in 2002/03.

Around 1999, five of the former Project Mercury Mk.1 staff and generator coaches also passed into Balfour Beatty's ownership, these having spent much of the decade with British Rail Telecommunications (BRT) but were sold off after the company was purchased by Racal and ceased rail operations in 1997.

ABOVE: Now under Network Rail ownership but still Railtrack-branded, MPV DR98002 leads the piling rig formation south through Stafford on March 11, 2002, with sister vehicle DR98001 at the rear. The KFA flat wagon is carrying mast foundations while the staff coach is BDC977168, The Mk.1s were only found in some of the MPV sets, for example they were rarely included in the much longer wiring formations. Gareth Bayer

ABOVE: Eagle-eyed readers may spot something odd about the windows of BDC977168 in this closer look at Stafford on March 11, 2002. At some point in its earlier BRT ownership, the original windows were replaced by smaller units from a Class 101 DMU, allowing six to be fitted per side. Internally, the coach was completely open plan with the BSK compartments removed. The original project logo is still carried while the coach is today preserved at the Spa Valley Railway and restored to Project Mercury colours. Gareth Bayer

ABOVE: The last operational staff coach on the national system was BDC977165, which is seen at Rugby on July 3, 2006, just a few months from retirement. Sporting a new alliance logo, other external signs of the safety legislation under which the vehicles now had to operate were the 'Danger CO2 Fire Systems' lettering and the first aid kit symbol. Sold to the West Somerset Railway in 2013, it has now been restored as part of the line's dining set with the generator retained in order to power the train's systems. Mike Cubberley

48 www.keymodelworld.com

A home from home

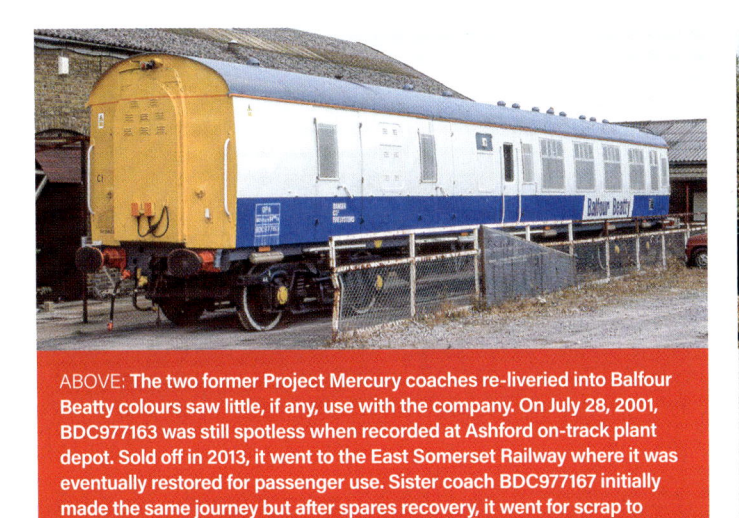

ABOVE: The two former Project Mercury coaches re-liveried into Balfour Beatty colours saw little, if any, use with the company. On July 28, 2001, BDC977163 was still spotless when recorded at Ashford on-track plant depot. Sold off in 2013, it went to the East Somerset Railway where it was eventually restored for passenger use. Sister coach BDC977167 initially made the same journey but after spares recovery, it went for scrap to Booth's the same year. *Gareth Bayer*

ABOVE: On an unrecorded date in 2000, a weather-beaten 09019 in Mainline Freight blue passes through the staff halt at Hoo Junction with two of the former Chipman weedkiller coaches in tow. Looking spotless in Balfour Beatty colours, they are, in order, CC99018 and CC9017. After their short-lived use on infrastructure workings, CC99017 was sold to the Buckinghamshire Railway Centre in 2002 while CC99018 went to the Wynward Woodland Park, near Stockton, during 2003 to become an educational room. *Simon Bendall Collection*

Two of this quintet, BDC977163 and BDC977167, were re-liveried into Balfour Betty colours and then proceeded to do little but keep a siding warm at Ashford until disposal in 2013.

The other three, BDC977165/66 and BDC977168, were more gainfully employed, being used on the ill-fated West Coast Route Modernisation project of the 2000s. This was conducted for Railtrack and then Network Rail by an alliance of infrastructure companies but would ultimately run late, go over budget and fail to deliver all of the planned improvements. The three Mk.1s operated with the small fleet of Windhoff Multi-Purpose Vehicles (MPVs) purchased specifically for the upgrade and provided staff facilities in certain formations. All were repainted in a very pale grey livery with BDC977165 remaining in use right up until 2006, thereby becoming the last traditional engineers' staff coach in use on the network.

Forming an alliance by Roland Turner

The chosen donor for this project to create West Coast Alliance staff and generator coach BDC977166 was a Bachmann Mk.1 BSK in InterCity livery; any release can be used but this one gave the correct Commonwealth bogies and no roof periscopes. Once stripped down, the end steps were partly removed, but the bottom one remained in place, as were the alarm gear, handrails, and gangway connections. The resultant marks were then sanded smooth and the hole above each gangway fitted with a piece of styrene sheet, filled, and made good. Holes for new end handrails were drilled and wire replacements fitted while the end toilet filler pipes should be retained

On the underframe, the battery boxes, dynamo, and vacuum cylinders were removed, and new parts added in the form of brake actuators (Hurst Models), a 3D-printed distributor (Shapeways) and an air cylinder (Southern Pride). I used 0.7mm wire to connect the brake actuators to the V-hangers. The gangway blanks were made from a piece of 20-thou plastic sheet that follows the shape of the Bachmann moulding and a second smaller 60-thou piece sized to fit within the confines of the first and with the top rounded off. The buffers were also replaced with extended versions from Comet Models while the external three-spoke handbrake wheels were from Wizard Models and painted before fitting.

The moulded roof vents were removed and replaced with the scallop style from MJT, while those over the former passenger area also have a revised layout that was copied using photos as a reference. The generator exhaust was made using a modified small Lima buffer! On the bodysides, the now sealed passenger doors had their handles and grabs removed and the guard's handrails replaced with 0.45mm wire.

The plated-over windows in the brake area were filled and rubbed down, with etched window frames from Hurst then fitted over the top to achieve the correct look. The mesh screens over the rest were cut from Scale-Link (sheet SLF060) and super-glued on, although an alternative mesh option is available from Southern Pride. Halfords white primer was used for the body colour, while the roof received BR diesel roof grey with a touch of white added to lighten it.

The transfers were home produced except for the electrification flashes while the glazing can be re-used where needed as it does not touch the mesh. Final details included end jumpers made from plastic and copper wire while the end alarms and solebar lights came from plastic off-cuts. Finally, the black stripes on the guard's door handrails can be done with paint or a black marker pen.

A home from home

Jarvis welfare coach

December 1999 saw Jarvis take delivery of a Fairmont Tamper P811-S track renewal machine at a cost of £10m, this being principally intended for use on the modernisation of the West Coast Main Line. Consisting of several elements, DR78901 as it was numbered was designed to unclip the existing track, recover the old sleepers and level the trackbed before then laying and spacing new sleepers and positioning the new rails, all in a single pass.

The first machine of its kind in the UK, it worked with a set of dedicated KRA sleeper carrying wagons with powered gantries running along the top of these to take new concrete sleepers to the machine for laying and remove the old ones. Tested during early 2000, it was subsequently placed into service, allowing track to be renewed at a rate never seen before in the UK.

Following a period of in-service experience, two support vehicles were added to the formation, the first around 2001 being a former KVA bogie ferry van built at Shildon Works in 1979. Previously numbered 33 70 2797 021-5 and originally owned by Danzas, this became tool van DC889400 with the TOPS code of YRA and finished in Jarvis maroon and grey.

Staff care

Then in early 2004, a converted Mk.3a sleeper was unveiled as an accompanying staff coach, or welfare coach in modern parlance, which could accommodate at least 24 people. Numbered DB977989 and with the TOPS code of QPA, modifications included mounting two diesel generator sets and accompanying fuel tanks on the underframe and installing a new electrical system. Completely rebuilt internally, the new facilities included a kitchen, storeroom, office/first aid room, two toilets, drying/washing room and a sizeable mess area with longitudinal tables, seats, and benches. Externally, the gangways were removed in favour of adjustable steel louvres while fold-down steps were fitted inside the doorways.

Finished in Jarvis colours, it was deployed into traffic from the spring of 2004 but proved to be something of an expensive white elephant as the track renewal train was stored at the beginning of 2006. By the middle of that year, the Jarvis logos had been replaced by those of subsidiary Fastline, but the coach remained out of use at York and then stored at MOD Bicester.

ABOVE: The Jarvis track renewal train is seen at Whitacre Junction on January 5, 2003, as 66515 powers the 6Y33 10.00 Stafford to Washwood Heath via Nuneaton with 66520 out of sight on the rear. The set had to regularly return to what was then RMC's sleeper facility for the accompanying wagons to be emptied of the recovered sleepers and new ones loaded. Leading the train is tool van DC889400 with the assorted parts of DR78901 behind. Scott Borthwick

Between 2008 md 2016, DB977989 was stored at the Railway Technical Centre, Derby, with sale to the Wensleydale Railway following, where it remains today in faded maroon. Meanwhile, DR78901 was exported to Italy in late 2008 while ferry van DC889400 also still exists, having gone to the East Lancashire Railway in 2018.

ABOVE: During 2021, Dapol released a new ready-to-run model of the Mk.3 sleepers in N gauge, the launch models including DB977989 in both versions of its maroon livery with either Jarvis or Fastline logos. The latter is illustrated with the model still featuring corridor connections, tooling costs understandably ruling out such one-off modifications.

LEFT: Still fresh from conversion by LH Group Services, DB977989 brings up the rear of the Jarvis track renewal train at Washwood Heath on June 8, 2004. With the generator sets hidden behind the underframe skirts, the external differences were largely limited to the ends but internally the coach was completely rebuilt.
Simon Stevens

A home from home

BR staff and tool vans

In addition to staff coaches, many cranes and some track machines that were normally hauled to worksites also ran with a tool van, this carrying assorted equipment and spares. As a step further, some vans were fully converted into staff vehicles, earlier types using 12-ton goods vans as their basis while, later on, more sophisticated conversions based around 22-ton ferry vans also emerged.

RIGHT: Originally built to diagram 1/218 as a 12-ton shock goods van, DB854782 was entirely typical of the ex-revenue vans found eking out their final years in support of a track machine, in this case Plasser and Theurer RM62 ballast cleaner DR76216. Seen at Watford Junction on June 30, 1984, it was accompanied by staff and dormitory coach DM395802. External 'alterations' amount to a 'D' added to the number, a new TOPS code of ZQV and faded chalk markings denoting its tool van role. Simon Bendall Collection

ABOVE: Occasionally, support wagons were given livery embellishments to mark them out as something different and not to be detached from their designated machine. However, someone had really gone to town on BR fish van DW87674 at Northampton on May 18, 1980, this notably not being one graced with the 'blue spot' designation as it lacks roller bearings. Assigned to London Midland Region ballast cleaner DR76219, it would last into the 1990s in this livery. Simon Bendall Collection

ABOVE: Seen at Horwich Works on August 16, 1980, DB771846 illustrates one of the 12-ton goods vans rebuilt as a staff and dormitory vehicle. Again for use with cranes and track machines, it was originally a plywood-bodied van to diagram 1/213 but the extensive work has seen two windows added in each end and one per side. Other alterations include a remodelled door, removed end vents, external hatch to house a gas bottle along with associated vent, and underframe steps. Simon Bendall Collection

ABOVE: The early 1990s saw several redundant 22-ton ferry vans rebuilt as staff and dormitory vans, these being commonly found accompanying Eastern Region machinery in the first half of the decade. Again, the work was considerable with the large door replaced by new bodywork with windows, and a personal door cut into each side along with a gas bottle locker. Green was the usual livery as seen on ZQX DB787148 with ballast cleaner DR76305 at Low Fell in September 1991. Mark Saunders

ABOVE: Page 8 provided a first look at the two BR ferry vans rebuilt into staff vans at York in 1994 and unusually taken into the departmental coaching stock series as LDB977922 and LDB977923. Just six months after that photo, the first of these vans is seen at Leeman Road on December 6, 1994, in an entirely different livery. The grey and blue had gone in favour of Powertrack light blue while the van sports a fire exit door that was another sign of the impact of health and safety rules. Mark Saunders

Modelling BR Departmental Coaching Stock

A home from home

BR staff brake vans

It was not just goods vans that became staff and dormitory vehicles, the same also occurred to a number of brake vans. The level of modification varied considerably from nothing at all to removed duckets and right through to an extensive rebuild with altered sides and ends. The illustrated examples are all from the 1980s, but examples could still be found running in the final years of British Rail.

RIGHT: Illustrating the most basic approach of 'touch nothing but some paint', LMS brake van DM731280 was the companion vehicle to yellow fish van DW87674 shown on the previous page. Again seen at Northampton on May 18, 1980, it has received yellow highlights and additional lettering of varying quality. The daubed on 'Do not detach from ballast cleaner 41' in yellow is particularly fetching while the more professional stencilled white lettering reads 'DCE depot ballast train'. Simon Bendall Collection

ABOVE: From the 'remove the duckets' category of conversions is another LMS example, DM731213 being recorded at Horwich Works on August 16, 1980. The ducket has been replaced by a window with a gas vent also installed below it, the TOPS code reading ZPO to denote its staff role. Otherwise, the van displays no external changes. The removal of duckets was also seen on some conversions of BR brake vans, examples including some taken into the Satlink fleet. Simon Bendall Collection

ABOVE: Some regulation BR orange curtains appear to have been purloined for this staff and dormitory conversion of DW35410, recorded at Cardiff Central on July 6, 1980, when working with 1961-built diesel-electric crane DRS81258. This was one of the final GWR-numbered Toad brake vans to be built and also displays a gas vent cut into the bodyside. The lettering states 'Sleeping and mess van for crane No. 358', which was the previous identity of this Smith-built example. Simon Bendall Collection

ABOVE: Built to diagram AA13 in the mid-1910s, DW17923 depicts the full staff and dormitory rebuild given to some Toads with the verandah now fully enclosed with horizontal wooden planking and a full height door installed. Meanwhile, the rest of the wooden planking has been replaced by steel sheeting with additional diagonal strengthening struts. An underframe gas bottle locker with 'No naked lights' warning is fitted with the ZPV recorded at Margam on October 13, 1981. Simon Bendall Collection

ABOVE: Another full staff and dormitory rebuild is seen at Newport Godfrey Road on February 26, 1983, this one being DB950575, which was one of the Toads built to diagram 1/502 by BR. This is smartly finished in olive green with cream lettering and displays a different style of conversion with the original planking still retained and more windows added in different positions. Unlike its sister, this one is not vacuum-braked, being unfitted with a through vacuum pipe as a ZPP. Simon Bendall Collection

A Toad staff conversion by Hywel Thomas

ABOVE: The staff and dormitory Toad awaits its next duty. The transfers were a mix of Railtec, Modelmaster and an old Woodhead Models sheet.

The Western Region made considerable use of brake van conversions for engineering duties and numerous Toads were altered over the years. These could often see extensive modifications with a closed off verandah and additional windows. The interiors varied depending on the needs of the owning department but often included bunks, desks, tool cupboards and cooking facilities.

The starting point for this 4mm scale model was Oxford Rail's rendition of a diagram AA3 van. As with several of the manufacturer's products, the basic moulding is excellent but rather let down by a number of irritating errors. Among other things, the lower planked ends should be sheet steel while the end windows are also wrong. An excellent article by Gerry Beale in *Model Railway Journal* No.268 showed how to correct these issues. I followed his lead by opening out the end windows and then adding new plastic to bring them to the correct four-plank depth. The ends were corrected by fitting very thin slivers of plastic between the planks and adding a five-thou sheet overlay. I replicated these alterations at the verandah end which, of course, was infilled on the mess van conversions.

It was then time to focus on the new door and window on each side. A similar technique was used to fill in the unwanted planks as this prevents the thin sheet overlays from sinking into the slots when solvent is applied. The two new windows were carefully cut out, followed by the door overlay and the window framing. A rainstrip was provided over the doors and windows along with a new stove chimney on the roof and a row of vents.

Rivet counting

Usually with wagon projects, I use slivers of plastic rod as rivets but as the Oxford mouldings were so fine, I thought a different approach might be in order to match them. I bought a sheet of Archer rivet transfers, which are not cheap but seem to be well defined compared to alternatives. This was the first time I had used them and, while fiddly, once mastered they really are excellent and a fine match for the moulded originals.

Moving on to the chassis, a major issue was the annoying current tendency of many RTR manufacturers to use non-standard axle lengths. After looking at the original wheels, I wondered whether I could file down the flanges and open the gauge out to EM. Each axle, minus one wheel, was put into a mini drill and the flange gently reduced with a fine file. With all four done, it was tested through my pointwork and ran without any issues.

With the chassis running, I turned my attention to the detailing. The mess vans only had steps beneath the doors, and these were created using the original mouldings cut down. The wagon-style brake gear was made up from a mix of metal castings, modified plastic kit parts and laminated strip. The final task was to add glazing and some curtains. By 1972, BR seemed to be using up a job lot of bright orange curtains in their engineering stock and these add a welcome splash of colour to the all-black van.

Lettering came from various sources, and it was numbered as DW301, which had been allocated to Neath, and would have been a regular sight in the Port Talbot area where my layout is set. With a through vacuum pipe and some new couplings, it was ready to enter service and is now a regular sight at Morfa Bank awaiting weekend engineering duties.

ABOVE: The Oxford model is seen after rebuilding the windows and fitting the new additions at the verandah end. The planks have been carefully scribed to match the original profile and depth. The side door is marked out and ready for the next stage.

ABOVE: The Archer rivet transfers after fixing to the sides, these providing a good match for the Oxford originals and far easier than using small slivers of plastic rod. With the primer applied, they are virtually indistinguishable from the mouldings.

A home from home

Instruction and Office coaches

Complementing the staff coaches was a diverse collection of other vehicles related to staff matters. These were generally less mobile and outright static in some instances but were not classified as internal users officially. The terms applied to them were varied such as office coach, training coach or instruction coach. The latter phrase was a particular favourite that could cover all manner of eventualities, such as vehicles sent to the Fire Training College at Moreton-in-Marsh or even those despatched to MOD Moreton-on-Lugg for the SAS to practice storming! A small selection of more regular uses is illustrated here that would be perfect for filling a corner of a yard or depot.

ABOVE: With 1993 bringing the introduction of secondary door locks for InterCity Mk.2s and Mk.3s, large numbers of staff needed to be trained on how to use them. To facilitate this, three redundant Mk.2e TSOs were suitably modified, renumbered as ADB977867- 69 and coded QXA. These training coaches were sent to key locations across the InterCity network, progressively moving to a new station as training was completed. ADB977869 covered the East Coast Main Line and Scotland but, as privatisation took effect, it was abandoned in Doncaster West Yard where it spent the latter half of the 1990s, being recorded on May 18, 1999. Taken on by Network Rail, it subsequently saw test train use as a radio survey vehicle but today serves as the support coach for Network Rail's Winter Development Vehicle, or hot-air blower for clearing points, and is normally found at Perth. Simon Bendall

RIGHT: There was some irony to DE320709 being branded as a mobile office when recorded at Barnetby permanent way depot on May 2, 1981, as it was sitting on a completely isolated section of track! Built in 1910, it was a Third Open for the Great Central Railway and would pass into the National Collection in 1983, Since then it has been on loan to the Great Central Railway with some restoration carried out but is now stored undercover. Trevor Mann

54 www.keymodelworld.com

A home from home

ABOVE: In tatty condition and covered in football-related graffiti, a tired DM395455 was captured at Watford Junction engineers' yard on June 4, 1981, when allocated to the Operating Department as an instruction coach. Officially, the prefix was TDM but just DM was physically displayed. Built in 1916, it was originally a ward car in an ambulance train before conversion into a Full Brake for the London & North Western Railway after the end of World War One. Taken into departmental stock in 1958, preservation came some 40 years later but, after bouncing around a number of locations, the bodywork was broken up in 2012 and the underframe used under the body of a royal saloon originally built for Queen Victoria in 1885. Simon Bendall Collection

ABOVE: The Southern Region had several office coaches on its books, including ADS70040 which was assigned to the Mechanical and Electrical Engineers. Originally a Maunsell Brake Third Corridor built in 1925, the coach then became the General Manager's instruction saloon in 1959. By May 17, 1980, it was in a rather less grandiose role at Haywards Heath but sporting a smart coat of olive green. Observed at other southern locations in surrounding years, it was scrapped in 1986. Simon Bendall Collection

ABOVE LEFT AND ABOVE RIGHT: A handful of the Metro-Cammell Mk.1 Pullman cars found their way into departmental service, but Pullman First Kitchen E314E *Hawk* was an unlikely choice to become M&EE instruction coach ADB975876 in 1979. Based at Oxley carriage sidings for a time, it was used to instruct London Midland staff in the intricacies of coach bogie design. To achieve this, it was accompanied by ADB935709, this being a vacuum-braked plate wagon built to diagram 1/434. This had a BR1 bogie, as initially used under Mk.1 coaches, mounted atop it along with a large tool container. Safety rails were also installed to allow staff to walk around the bogie. Both are seen at Chester carriage and wagon sidings on April 17, 1982. Although delivered to Vic Berry's Leicester yard at some point in 1988 for scrapping, plans to potentially re-use the Pullman saw it set aside but disposal eventually came three years later. Trevor Mann

ABOVE: Even in the privatisation era, redundant coaches have seen use as training vehicles, being used to conduct emergency evacuation exercises for example. This has included Mk.2d TSO 5636, which has resided at St Philip's Marsh depot in Bristol for over a decade. In the BR era, such vehicles would have been renumbered as an internal user, but this practice was abandoned some 25 years ago. Seen at the depot open day on May 2, 2016, it was offered for sale three years later but remains in place in early 2022. Simon Bendall

ABOVE: The other static coach used by Great Western at its Bristol depot was a Mk.1, which in recent years has gone by its original identity of 4598. However, for the bulk of its life it had been cinema coach ZDB975403, which was converted in 1974 for use by BR's publicity and public relations department. This could be included in travelling exhibition trains or used in a static role at trade exhibitions and open days. The early 1990s saw it assume a static role at Bristol Bath Road TMD, moving to St Philip's Marsh when this depot closed. Having carried various Great Western liveries over the years, it was preserved at the Swindon and Cricklade Railway in 2019 for conversion back to passenger use. It is seen, more or less, at the 'Marsh' during the 2016 open day. Simon Bendall

Consett Ore Wagon

Today we launch our latest wagon. Having had this suggested to us and following a poll on our Facebook page, we are going to produce the 56t Iron Ore Wagon, used in Consett.

Available in OO and N. Delivery is expected 3rd Qtr 2021. Prices are 3 pack £67.00 and 9 pack £199.00

A brief look at the Tyne Dock - Consett iron ore workings Class 9F's 92060 - 92066 & 92097 - 92099 Class 24's 24102 – 24111

https://www.krmodels.co.uk/products/consett-iron-ore-wagon

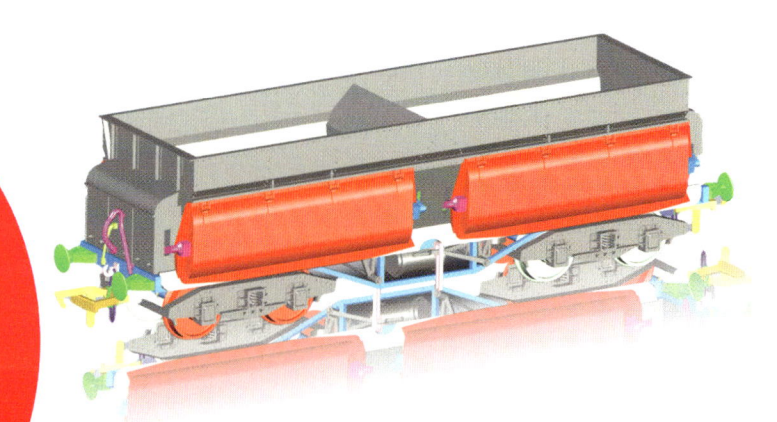

www.krmodels.co.uk

KRModels

The Palbrick B Wagon OO Gauge

The Palbrick Wagon dates back to the mid 1950's, seeking to replace the ancient brick wagons used by LNER.

Originally medium goods wagons converted to carry pallets of bricks, the Palbrick featured 3 different variations for different sizes of pallets. Palbrick A could carry 13 tons, whereas B and C could carry 16 tons.

Across all of the roughly 1400 Palbrick wagons that were made, all of them had some changes or variations to them that differed from the standard templates.

By the 1960's, most of the had fallen out of use and converted into other types of wagons. Some converted into match wagons, others into shellcase wagons. Now, very few exist across the UK.

We will produce both body shapes of the Palbrick B wagon, the most common.

Available 1qtr 2022
3 car rake for £60.00
plus shipping

Order now from
www.krmodels.co.uk/products/oo-gauge

Stores on the move

Stores on the move

Much like the staff coaches, stores vehicles came in a wide range of types and with a variety of roles. David Ratcliffe takes a look at a selection of these, beginning with the Enparts workings before considering the other vehicles belonging to the Mechanical and Electrical Engineers and then how BR moved its stationery around the network.

During the British Rail era, stores coaches conformed to three categories, those that moved regularly, as needed or were static. The latter were typically considered as internal user vehicles and numbered as such, leaving the other two types as departmental coaching stock.

Most of the engineering departments had a quantity of stores vehicles on their books but in terms of coaches, it was the Mechanical and Electrical Engineers that dominated. This was largely due to the Civil Engineers and Signal and Telegraph Engineers making use of considerable numbers of former 12-ton goods vans for their purposes, not that the M&EE was particularly lacking here either.

It was the Enparts network, an abbreviation for engine parts, that made much use of the M&EE coaching stock fleet throughout BR's corporate era, these being supplemented by a number of specially adapted wagons assigned to particular roles. Moving stores around the country did not generate money to pay for the upkeep of the fleet though, nor was the stock compatible with the Speedlink air-braked wagonload network.

While smaller consignments were moved to Speedlink using surplus air-braked wagons, the transport of bulky items such as engines and bogies could not, and this was switched to the roads during the 1980s as BR looked to cut its costs. Inevitably, smaller parts would follow suit during the early 1990s.

ABOVE: Former BR fish van DB975388 was lettered as being assigned to the Eastern Region for use as a stores van in the Civil Engineers-operated weedkilling train. However, on July 14, 1979, it was in a different role at Southend Central delivering fixtures and fittings to the newly refurbished station. The lengthy train included all manner of 12-ton vans transferred to the Civil Engineers, including shock vans and some of pre-nationalisation origin, like W145605 next along and lacking a 'D' prefix. DB975388 would be scrapped at Shildon in 1983. Simon Bendall Collection

ABOVE: The late 1980s and early 1990s saw the Signal and Telegraph Engineers take on several stores coaches as the department was involved in a number of re-signalling projects. These were generally short-lived and unchanged but considerable attention was lavished on three Mk.1 GUVs in 1990 as they were assigned to the high-profile installation of Automatic Train Protection at the London end of the Great Western Main Line. TOPS coded QRV, KDB977556-58 were given full repaints into the then new Satlink red and yellow livery and lettering applied stating their ATP dedication. In the event though, their use on the main line was very short, lasting just a matter of months before transfer to static use at Reading and Bristol, this bringing renumbering as internal users 061205-07. Brightening up an otherwise dull day, one of these GUVs was included in the 6C11 13.13 Gloucester-Taunton Fairwater behind 50042 Triumph on July 3, 1990, when approaching Cam & Dursley station. The formation otherwise features YCV Turbot, ZBV Grampus and ZKV Barbel wagons. RTR models of these GUVs have been produced in OO gauge by both Lima and Bachmann and in N gauge by Graham Farish. Martin Loader

Stores on the move

Enparts traffic

ABOVE: **Vintage Mink D ADW198 is recorded in internal use at Swindon Works on May 19, 1979, long after its withdrawal from main line Enparts traffic. It had managed to acquire a TOPS code of ZRV though.** Paul Bartlett

BELOW: **Enparts vans could often be found formed in regular parcels trains, this offering a cost effective means of moving the vehicles around the region. Seen around 1970, former GWR Fruit C DW150356 was in such a working when recorded at Bath. It is now preserved at Didcot.**
53A Models of Hull Collection/John Senior

The carriage of M&EE stores such as locomotive spare parts between main workshops and motive power depots was a long-standing rail movement and, over the years, a wide range of vehicles that were no longer required for revenue service would be used on these workings.

Known as Enparts traffic on the Western Region, which was a term first coined by the Great Western Railway, its stores fleet had included four-wheel vans as well as bogie vehicles. Among them were nine 18ft wheelbase Mink D dating from 1911, which had replaced a number of even earlier six-wheel Siphon milk vans in the traffic in 1944. Renumbered as DW198-206, they would in turn be replaced during the 1960s, when the stores fleet was enlarged to include two 12ft wheelbase Fruit C, several 18ft wheelbase Fruit D and four bogie Siphon G. However, the various four-wheel vans were restricted to a maximum speed of either 45 or 50mph. As a result, they would be removed from main line service by 1968, after which they were to be found at Swindon Works moving equipment internally around the site.

In 1970, ten redundant BR Mk.1 BSO coaches were added to the Western Region's Enparts fleet, becoming ADB975034-43, while they were joined the following year by a couple of 1935-built Collett 57ft Full Brakes

Modelling BR Departmental Coaching Stock 59

Stores on the move

ABOVE: ADB975157 was one of the two Collett Full Brakes transferred to Enparts use in 1971, having been built in 1935. Seen at Swindon Works on May 19, 1979, its lettering includes the instruction 'Not to work off Western Region.' This is another van still surviving today, this time at the Cholsey and Wallingford Railway. Paul Bartlett

ABOVE: Over the years, the Siphon G vans have become somewhat synonymous with Enparts traffic despite them being only part of the overall fleet. Looking smart in olive green, ADB975784 was recorded at Reading on July 24, 1982, it being lettered to work between the depot and Swindon Works. This was a BR-built example from 1951, to diagram O62 and with its original sliding vents plated over along the lower bodyside. Accurascale will be releasing an extensive range of Siphon G models in OO gauge during 2022. Paul Bartlett

RIGHT: Representing the Mk.1 Enparts coaches is former BSK ADB975647 at Plympton on June 6, 1979. While the initial BSO conversions were sometimes repainted, the later transfers tended to remain in BR blue/grey. In poor external condition and with minimal extra branding, this example would be scrapped by Marple & Gillott of Sheffield in April 1982. Paul Bartlett

ABOVE AND LEFT: One of the BR Mk.1 BGs used to carry HST parts from Derby Loco Works to Bristol, ADB975613 was stabled at Bristol Temple Meads on July 12, 1980. After its use in Enparts traffic ended, this coach was converted into a tool van for the Old Oak Common breakdown train. It was eventually scrapped in 2011. Bachmann has produced a model of this particular BG in both its OO and Graham Farish N gauge ranges, the former being pictured. Simon Bendall Collection

Stores on the move

ABOVE: The fleet of 16 Siphon G vans used to transfer seating material between Derby and Swindon were all given the rarely used CDB prefix to their departmental numbers, this denoting vehicles allocated to traffic from the British Railway Engineering Limited (BREL) workshops. CDB975854 is seen at Swindon Works on October 5, 1980. This was one of the very last Siphons to be built in 1955 and retains all of its side ventilators but had lost its corridor connections while in previous revenue use. *Simon Bendall Collection*

ABOVE: The Siphons allocated to the seat material traffic were a mix of GWR and BR built examples and the conversions that existed within them. For example, CDB975856 was from the 1951-built BR batch and had previously been assigned to newspaper packing duties as evidenced by the plated over bodyside vents. Seen at Swindon on June 6, 1981, the gangway bellows were likely removed upon entering departmental use, leaving the connecting door in-situ. *Simon Bendall Collection*

RIGHT: Originally built by the GWR in 1936, CDB975838 was one of over 50 Siphons converted three years later into casualty evacuation coaches in preparation for potential German air raids and later in the war served overseas in an ambulance train. The main aspect of the conversion was the removal of the body vents and addition of windows alongside the internal alterations. The van is seen at Derby Litchurch Lane on August 11, 1979 and would be scrapped in 1986; all of the Siphons in this BREL traffic suffering the same fate around this time. *Simon Bendall Collection*

from diagram K41, which were renumbered as ADB975157/58. Further Mk.1 transfers then followed, all being BSKs, with the pair of ADB975138/39 from 1971 and the quintet of ADB975643-47 in 1977.

In 1976, four BR Mk.1 BGs also moved to Enparts traffic, primarily for the carriage of HST spares between BREL's workshops at Derby and Doncaster and the depots at Bristol, Laira, and Old Oak Common, while in 1978 some 18 Siphon G were renumbered as ADB975774-91 and also added to the Enparts pool. The following year, a further 16 Siphon G joined them, with these being primarily intended to carry seat trim material between the works at Derby Litchurch Lane and Swindon.

However, the transfer of M&EE stores traffic to the air-braked Speedlink freight network in the early 1980s made the Enparts fleet redundant and most of the vehicles were then either scrapped or went into internal use. Some of the Mk.1 coaches would find further use in departmental service though, most notably the BGs which were re-deployed as tool vans with the Breakdown Train Unit.

ABOVE: Enparts vehicles were a common sight in the West Country, moving to and from Laira depot, Plymouth. This was achieved using regular wagonload services as seen on July 21, 1980, as 50002 *Superb* powers into the summer evening with a Tavistock Junction to Exeter Riverside service at Langford Bridge. Leading the formation is an Enparts Siphon with two well wagons behind. The first one is carrying a complete Class 50 bogie while another is the likely load beneath the sheeting on the second wagon. The rest of the train includes liquid petroleum gas and Class A petroleum tankers, cement presflos and a small number of 12-ton vans, among others. *Peter Gray/Antony Guppy*

Modelling BR Departmental Coaching Stock **61**

Stores on the move

A trio of Enparts conversions by Hywel Thomas

Rebuilt from an Ian Kirk kit, Fruit C DW150356 is seen on the author's Morfa Bank Sidings.

By 1972, which is the date my EM gauge layout is set, the Enparts fleet consisted of around 34 vans. This included Mink D, some of which had been replaced by Fruit D with the same numbers, a Mink D that retained its original number of DW28797 and two Fruit C. There were also four Siphon G with more following later, three more Fruit D, a pair of former GWR Post Office stowage vans, a pair of diagram K41 BGs, and a single former Southern BY, which was involved in an accident during April 1971 and may have not been repaired. Mk.1 additions included a fleet of eight BSOs from 1969 that carried a range of liveries from olive green to blue and grey plus a few patch-painted examples, and finally two Mk.1 BSKs converted at Newton Abbot in 1971.

The first of these vans to be tackled was one of the two Fruit C in the fleet, which were numbered DW150355/56. There are no current models for the Fruit C but Ian Kirk did produce the similar Mink C many years ago. These occasionally turn up but always fetch very inflated prices so I was resigned to either waiting for a new kit or scratchbuilding one. Then, during a foray into the loft, I was pleasantly surprised to discover a dusty example built about 1979 and long forgotten!

It was quickly dusted off and examined with a view to a rebuild as an Enparts van. Fortunately, the model soon came apart as the glue had gone brittle after so many years in a partly insulated loft. The Fruit C was actually six inches longer and with a 12ft 6in wheelbase compared to the Mink C but I decided I could live with that as the Kirk body mouldings were still rather nice.

The ends were discarded and replaced with Ratio examples from its GWR 12-ton van kit. The outside-framed doors were then filled in with 60-thou sheet offcuts ahead of rebuilding as the later, more familiar, inside-framed variety. The new doors were then made from 10-thou overlays with other strip used for the detailing. The rivets came from an Archer transfer sheet. Some ABS whitemetal brake parts were added underneath and the original roof fettled to fit the Ratio ends and fixed in place. Finally, the footboards were made from various thicknesses of strip. These were supported by split-pins that had been opened out flat and bent to shape using an etch folder.

After a coat of primer, the van was ready for painting. This van did run in either freight brown or a very dirty crimson until around 1970 but when I found the original some years later, it was in very faded olive green. I decided to paint it in the latter livery but as freshly painted in 1972, so weathering was kept to a minimum. Transfers were a mix of various brands along with some I made specifically for the model.

Additional vehicles

Although only a single Enparts van will appear on the layout at any one time, I wanted a few other types so I could ring the changes for variety. The next addition was a straightforward build of a Parkside Fruit D plastic kit. This was going to represent one of the DW198-206 number series. Originally, this series was made up of six-wheel Siphon milk vans but these had been replaced from 1947 by a group of Mink D vans that took the same numbers. Four of these were themselves supplanted by Fruit D vans from 1971 and a photo of one of these, DW206 at Canton in 1973, provided the inspiration.

Parkside kit PC74 was soon on the workbench and built exactly as per the instructions with the wheels opened out to EM gauge. This van would have been getting on for a year old when my layout is set so once again featured quite a clean olive green livery and some custom-designed transfers to replicate the Canton photo.

The final member, so far, of my Enparts fleet was one of the 1969 conversions from redundant Mk.1 BSO coaches. A Hornby BR maroon example had been purchased a while back when it was going fairly cheap so it was moved onto the workbench. Two of the fleet are known to have carried their original maroon livery, one with extensive olive green patch painting. When first

Stores on the move

ABOVE LEFT: **The Ian Kirk Mink C van as discovered in the loft after removing the roof and ends. Some salvaged Ratio ends await test fitting to see if the conversion was feasible.**

ABOVE RIGHT: **The doors of the model undergoing modification to the later inside-framed type.**

LEFT: **With the new doors almost completed on the Fruit C conversion, the missing rib bases have been fitted along with the nameboard and other details. It would then be painted and finished as per the opening picture.**

taken into the fleet, many still had their windows intact, simply losing their seating but soon windows were either painted over or replaced. My example, DB975039, was still in maroon livery when noted at Landore some five years after conversion but all of the windows were overpainted.

Minimal structural changes were made to the original Hornby model with just the removal of the end steps and swapping the wheels. On the prototype, several doors had been repainted, perhaps replaced by examples in better condition, and these had been painted maroon but without lining. This was replicated on the model along with a single grey painted window on one side and two on the other. Various scratches

RIGHT: **The route to the larger Fruit D is much simpler, being a straightforward build of the Parkside kit. This is finished in reasonably clean olive green as converted in late 1971.**

LEFT: **The Hornby BSO was virtually out of the box with painted-over windows along with some scratches and missing lining to represent its run-down condition.**

were painted on using a fine brush and, after removing the original numbers, new transfers were added to suit. Finally, some heavy weathering and it was ready to join the fleet.

Future additions will see a Mink D (another Parkside kit), possibly one of the 1971 conversions from a Mk.1 BSK and also a Siphon G, either a Lima rebuild or a new Accurascale example when they appear. The Enparts fleet certainly makes an interesting group and can legitimately be added to any Western parcels train for some variety.

Modelling BR Departmental Coaching Stock 63

Stores on the move

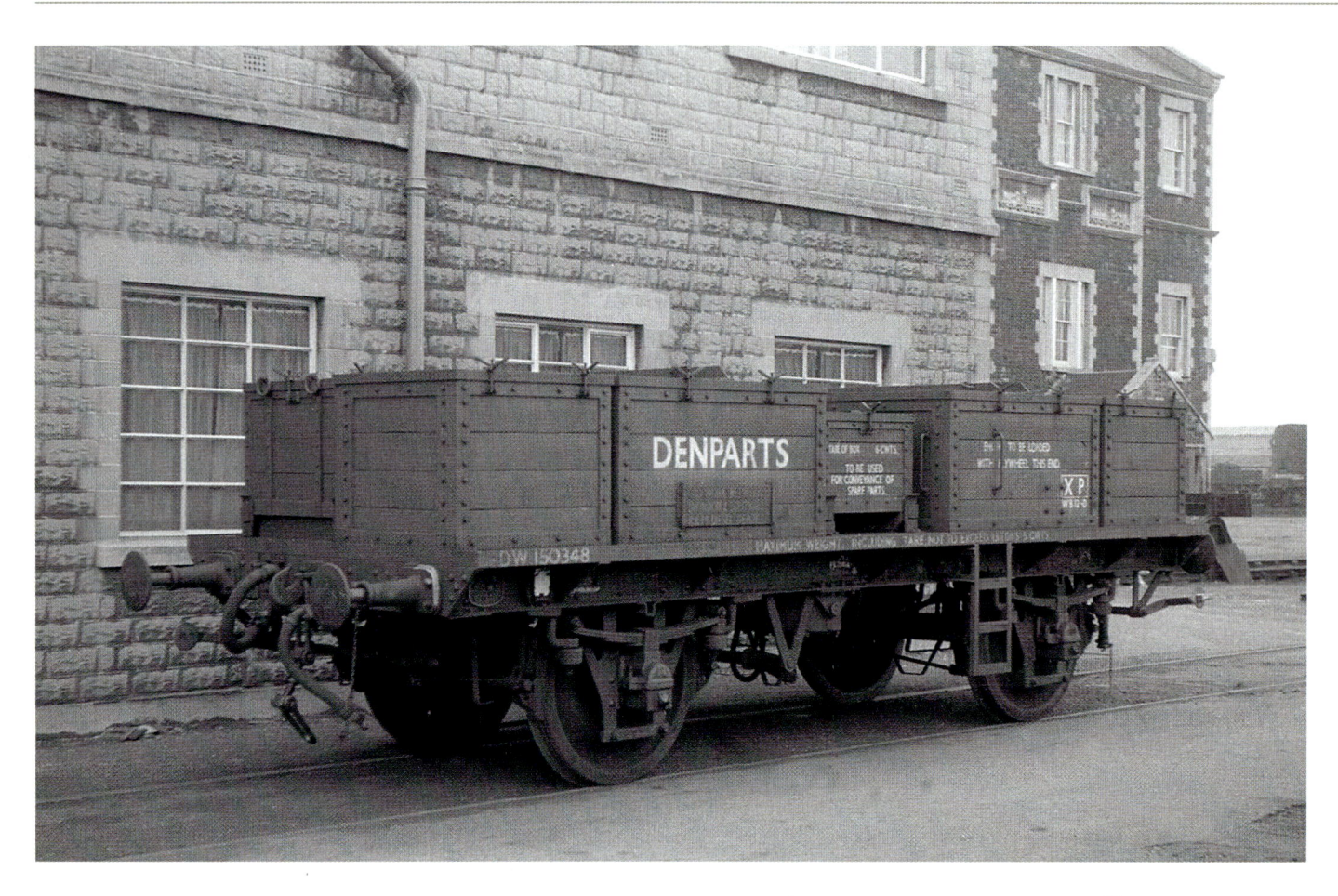

Denparts and Denflats

The Western Region was also the first to develop the Denparts wagons, as in diesel engine parts, when in 1959/60, it modified at least nine horsebox chassis (eight GWR and one LNER design) by removing the bodies and fitting wooden storage boxes to the floor. The first three were fitted with four boxes, incorporating two larger boxes situated towards the middle of the floor flanked by a smaller box either side, while some of the later conversions were fitted with more boxes of differing sizes. All were lettered 'Denparts' and used to convey DMU engines and gearboxes that had been overhauled at Swindon Works back to the various DMU depots around the region.

In addition to its Denparts fleet, the Western also converted at least 14 Conflat A wagons, ten ex-GWR and four BR, into three types of Denflat. This involved fitting specially designed frames to the floors of the vacuum-braked wagons with the Denflat E, of which there were at least four, being used to convey Maybach engines while the Denflat T could carry two transmission types. The Denflat E and T were all conversions of ex-GWR Conflats and worked from Swindon Works on specific planned schedules, while the four Denflat B, as converted from BR Conflats, were used to carry various loads between Derby and Swindon. Most of the Denflats were withdrawn following the

ABOVE: **Most of the Western Region's Denparts wagons were converted from GWR diagram N13 horseboxes. DW150348 is pictured at Swindon Works around 1967 with its various lettering including 'Denparts to work between Swindon Works and diesel depot', 'To be used for conveyance of spare parts' and 'Engine to be loaded with flywheel this end'. The Western's Denparts fleet was withdrawn in the late 1970s with this example scrapped at Barry in 1984.** Simon Bendall Collection

RIGHT: **Former GWR Conflat ADW39860, now a Denflat E and coded ZRV, is pictured at Severn Tunnel Junction Yard on May 29, 1985. It would most likely have been en route from Swindon Works to Laira depot.** Trevor Mann

Stores on the move

demise of the Class 52 Westerns in 1976, but one or two would last in departmental service into the mid-1980s.

Working alongside the Denflats were four Weltrol WP, modified by the fitting of wooden supports in the well and which were used to carry diesel locomotive bogies, as pictured on page 61. There was also a vacuum-braked ex-LMS plate wagon that was modified to carry Class 08 wheelsets from Swindon to the heavy maintenance depots at Bristol Bath Road, Cardiff Canton, Plymouth Laira, and Swansea Landore.

Expansion

The Denparts concept was also taken up by the London Midland Region, although it chose to modify 40 vacuum-braked 10ft wheelbase LMS and BR medium open wagons (Medfits) by removing the bodies and fitting three wooden boxes to the floor. Recoded ZRV, in total 22 LMS and 18 BR Medfits were converted for Denparts traffic from BREL Derby Loco Works and, until 1981, they could be seen working to DMU depots across the London Midland, Eastern and North Eastern regions. Also in Denparts traffic from Crewe and Derby to Scottish depots were former LMS BG ADB975562 and LMS 42ft GUV ADB975560. Both were recoded QRV, but they had been removed from Denparts traffic by 1980.

Somewhat longer lived were the four wagons built for the Southern Region at Ashford in 1957/58 to carry DEMU engines between Eastleigh Works and St Leonards depot at Hastings. Numbered ADB998050-53, these 13-ton flats had a small tool locker at either end with the engine sitting between them on a fabricated floor fitted with mounting points so that the engine could be securely bolted-down.

When the wagons were first introduced, the load was simply covered with tarpaulin sheets but after a few years, rounded steel covers were provided to be placed over the top to prevent water and other damage, their appearance earning them the nickname 'Singer' after the sewing machines. When built, the four were vacuum-braked but subsequently through air pipes were fitted with at least two then fully converted to air brakes.

ABOVE: Lying condemned at Swindon Works on May 19, 1979, Denflat E ADW39399 still has a Maybach diesel engine mounted on it. With the tarpaulin removed, the supporting structure to which the engine was secured for transport can be seen. Paul Bartlett

ABOVE: One of the London Midland's Denparts wagons is seen at Darlington North Yard on April 6, 1980, ZRV ADM476958 being lettered 'Return to Derby Loco Works.' Trevor Mann

BELOW: QRV ADB975560 was photographed at Derby Litchurch Lane on August 11, 1979, with its 'Denparts ScR' lettering barely discernible beneath the layers of dirt. This former LMS 42ft GUV had been transferred to the M&EE fleet in 1975 and worked between Glasgow and Derby. By 1985, it was in use as a stores van at Aberdeen Ferryhill TMD before passing into preservation at Brechin. Today it is located at the Royal Deeside Railway. Simon Bendall Collection

ABOVE: The four Southern DEMU engine carriers were built to diagram 1/635 at Ashford with DB998052 recorded at Eastleigh Works around 1970. All four of ADB998050-53, now with amended prefix, were transferred to internal user status in the early 1990s, becoming 083651-54. Only one now survives, ADB998050 being owned by Hastings Diesels Ltd and confined to St Leonards depot while the pictured ADB998052 was scrapped at Eastleigh in October 2005. 53A Models of Hull Collection/John Senior

Modelling BR Departmental Coaching Stock 65

Stores on the move

Dabbling with Denparts by Hywel Thomas

DW150199 makes an appearance at Morfa Bank as part of a complex diagram that saw it marshalled in a freight from Swindon to Margam before joining the Morfa Bank trip. From there it would head back west to Canton on a Morfa Bank to Penarth Curve Sidings engineers' working.

The Western Region embarked on its dieselisation programme in the late 1950s, this included not only planning the fleets and depots in some detail but also the wagons that would be needed to deliver spares ranging from the smallest bracket up to entire diesel engines. Alongside the Enparts and Denflat fleets came the small group known as Denparts, which were built on horsebox underframes. Like the other fleets, they worked from Swindon to the larger depots carrying diesel parts, including DMU engines and gearboxes.

Converted from 1958 to 1962 and numbered within the Western's departmental series, there were just eight wagons in the pool. After an accident that wrote one of them off, a replacement conversion appeared in 1969, this using an ex-LNER underframe.

The large storage boxes covered the full width of the wagons but a view of one of these from above in 1968 shows two central square boxes while another view shows additional boxes across the ends so there were alterations over the years. By 1972, when Morfa Bank Sidings is set, the flats carried two full width large boxes and two smaller ones outside of these.

An obvious starting point was the 4mm scale Parkside range and so a pair of suitable chassis sprues were purchased from Peco. The two I had opted to model were DW150199, a former GWR N13 horsebox with Churchward brakes, and the 1969 replacement for the damaged wagon, DW150409. This was an ex-LNER diagram 5 horsebox built by the LMS on lot number 1675 but allocated to the Western as W2502E. The LNER chassis was for a different diagram so required lengthening by 8mm, but the GWR chassis was built as supplied. Both were fitted with 14mm coach wheels.

The boxes that carried the parts were the most obvious and distinctive feature of these wagons and they were tackled next. Several of the wagons I recorded at Woodham's scrapyard in Barry had already seen the wooden boxes burnt in order to recover the metal parts and these photos proved invaluable in working out the assembly of the framing.

A riveting time

Essentially, the models were just simple plastic sheet boxes that were scribed before assembly to represent the planked construction. Each included a false floor beneath which was filled with loose 'liquid lead' to add much needed weight. Two lifting shackles were fitted on the lids of the large boxes along with screw down fastenings on each edge. The shackles were made from brass wire and the fastenings used plastic strip bent to shape once dry. These were fiddly but worth the effort.

With the basic shapes complete, the matter of rivets became unavoidable. I did consider using the Archer rivet transfers to save me the tedious job of adding countless small pieces of plastic but the spacing was not quite right and I did not have enough in stock anyway so there was no escape.

I did one box as a test piece, partly to see how long it took and also to see if it was possible to get away without them. There was no avoiding it though as the box looked much more like the real thing with the rivets fitted as it was such a feature of the prototype designs. So, it was on with some good music, plenty of solvent, a sharp new scalpel blade and a steady hand! The task did take a while, but it was worth the effort once finished. All eight boxes were then sprayed with Halfords grey primer but not attached to the wagons as it was easier to paint the component parts before fitting them together.

This fleet carried various liveries, and mixes of liveries too, over the years, ranging from overall black when new and very possibly gulf red in the 1960s, but the ones I recorded were either in freight brown, patch painted with olive green or all over olive. I did wonder if they were still gulf red but one of the examples I photographed in Barry was alongside a standard 13-ton steel Highfit and the colours were identical.

I decided that my two were to carry freight brown and olive green for variety. The floors were finished as unpainted wooden planks and the underframes in dirty black. The transfers were created on the computer and specific to each wagon as they are a tight fit on the box sides and also very small along the side rails of each wagon. Once painted, the boxes were secured to the floors and each wagon given a coat of weathering. With couplings fitted, they were then ready for service on the layout.

Stores on the move

ABOVE: The two chassis before fitting the floors. The holes in the sub-frame allow solvent to reach the underside of the floor once fitted.

ABOVE: The Peco LNER chassis required lengthening to suit the original dimensions of the donor horsebox, which was achieved by adding Evergreen plastic strip in the centre.

ABOVE: In contrast, the GWR chassis was built as per the original instructions with both of them receiving etched steps in the appropriate positions.

ABOVE: The eight boxes are seen in completed form except for the rivets. Inside each one was a false floor creating a low box into which lead weights were fitted.

BELOW: The first riveted box is seen after the application of primer, this being completed in advance of the rest to gauge the overall look.

ABOVE: The other wagon, DW150409, illustrates the difference in length between this and those based on GWR chassis and also makes for an interesting variation. As a late addition to the fleet in 1969, it has been assumed that its livery would still be quite clean after just three years in operation.

Modelling BR Departmental Coaching Stock **67**

Stores on the move

M&EE stores vehicles

ABOVE: Type 1 20063 is at the head of a very mixed consist in the reception roads of Derby Locomotive Works on August 4, 1980. The front portion of the train features three of the former LMS six-wheel fish vans, which were coming towards the end of their service life. These are mixed with six of the Denparts wagons converted by the London Midland Region from Medfits. The back of the train is made up of a number of air-braked vans, including some VDAs, so with a mix of air and vacuum stock, the train would be running partially fitted with a brake van just discernible on the rear. Rail Photoprints

The stores of the Mechanical & Electrical Engineers department consisted of parts and spares predominately associated with locomotives, coaches, and wagons. For example, this included consumable items such as brake blocks, wagon springs and locomotive sand along with replacement parts such as buffers, couplings, brake valves, wagon sheets and much more. While wagons made up much of the fleet, a number of former parcels and other non-passenger coaches were also employed. A large proportion of the traffic was transferred to Speedlink in the early 1980s, but some vehicles remained in use as part of the Rolling Stock Engineer's division.

Prior to this, a significant part of the fleet consisted of over 40 vacuum-braked six-wheel fish vans that had been built to LMS diagram 2115 at Wolverton in 1949. These were re-allocated to the M&EE a decade later after six-wheeled vehicles were banned in passenger trains due to concerns about the ride characteristics of such stock.

Under the M&EE, they were used to move parts and stores such as the above from the BREL workshops at Crewe, Derby, and Horwich to depots across the network. These were repainted from crimson lake, first into black and later in olive green. At 31ft long and featuring two large sliding doors each side, they were popular with the engineers and remained in main line departmental service until 1980 or so. The last note of their operation to appear in the author's collection of TOPS train consists was the loaded movement of ADM40228 and ADM40254 from the loco stores at BREL Crewe to Willesden TMD on April 1, 1980. Some were then retained as static stores at Derby Works for a few more years.

LEFT: A closer look at one of the former fish vans sees ADM40316 stored in Doncaster Hexthorpe Yard on June 12, 1980. Coded QRV, the lettering at the far end states 'To be returned to loco stores, Derby' in addition to the allocation lettering beneath the number. A nice plastic kit of these vehicles is available in 4mm scale from Chivers Finelines. Trevor Mann

Stores on the move

RIGHT: The four dual-braked 14-ton bogie scenery vans of B889200-03 were built at Lancing Works in 1958 to diagram 1/292 for use on the Dover to Dunkerque train ferry. Similar in design to the prototype General Utility Van, they had two sets of side doors in addition to the end doors and were initially used to carry Rolls-Royce cars from Crewe to the continent. After their ferry use ended in 1981, they were recoded from VIX to YRX and joined the M&EE stores fleet, where they oversaw the movement of BRUTE parcels trolleys to New Cross Gate for repair, EMU spares from Eastleigh Works and new platform seats from Stewarts Lane. B889203, also numbered 21 70 2397 003-1, is pictured at South Lambeth freight depot in February 1979. Remarkably, all four still survive today, two at Stewarts Lane as stores vehicles for Belmond, which operates the British Pullman, and the other pair at the Mid Hants Railway, these arriving in June 2021 after many years stored at Eastleigh. Trevor Mann

ABOVE: Serving as companions to the four bogie scenery vans were the 30 motor car vans built to diagram 1/291 at Lancing at the same time. Despite their shorter length, they were also rated to carry 14-tons and again bore a close resemblance to the protype Mk.1 Covered Carriage Truck. Once their train ferry careers came to an end, many found an assortment of departmental roles, including conversion to staff coaches and use as barrier or stores vans. Overhauled a year earlier, ADB889014 was still looking smart in olive green when recorded at Hoo Junction on June 24, 1984. As dual braked vehicles, here coded ZRX, they were useful on the Southern Region where vacuum-only stock was frowned upon and this one formed part of the diverse Rolling Stock Engineers sub-fleet. This usefulness ensured they had quite long service lives, one even making it into Balfour Beatty white and blue as a ballast cleaner support van. Over half the fleet survives in preservation. Paul Bartlett

ABOVE: With the M6 motorway in the background, 25109 has just departed from Bescot Yard with a southbound Speedlink service in January 1987. Immediately behind the loco is one of the four former bogie scenery vans still fresh from overhaul with the very mixed consist then featuring a SPA steel open, two YGH Sealion ballast hoppers, a tanker hidden by the catenary mast, a through-piped 21-ton mineral wagon, and then a BDA bolster wagon. Simon Bendall Collection

Bachmann's Southern stores van

During 2016/17, Bachmann released several coaches and wagons in its OO gauge range finished in departmental condition. This included the Enparts Mk.1 BG illustrated in that section while another offering was the Southern CCT as a member of the M&EE's Rolling Stock Engineers fleet. The manufacturer managed to find an unmodified vehicle that matched the tooling in the form of ADB975276, which was a stores van based at Stewarts Lane. This was taken into departmental service in 1973 and relegated to internal user status 11 years later. It was subsequently preserved at the East Lancashire Railway but in 2021, it was repurposed as a glamping van in a field in Powys!

Modelling BR Departmental Coaching Stock

Stores on the move

M&EE ex ferry stores vans by Mark Lambert

ABOVE: This is the second of the ferry GUV conversions using thin plastic sides from a silhouette cutter overlaid on the Lima bodysides. This is finished as the last built of the scenery vans, ADB889203, following transfer to M&EE use and recoding as a YRX.

This 4mm scale project started with a chance find of a Mopok kit for the BR scenery vans, sometimes known as ferry GUVs on eBay. Mopok kits featured excellent whitemetal castings alongside a selection of early 1970s kit-building staples such as printed acetate sides, a wooden floor and vacuum-formed bodyshell together with various sizes of plastic strip to brace the sides and add details. After the best part of 50 years, much of the kit ended up in the spares box or the bin as the easiest way these days to produce a different sort of GUV is to glue the printed acetate sides onto a RTR shell.

I used a Lima GUV as a donor with the preparatory work being fairly brutal; the whole of each side needs to be filed flat to remove all of the detail and key the surface to take the glue. As the replacement sides were quite thick (about 20-thou), it pays to attack the plastic with a large file to reduce the width of the body slightly. I added handrails and door furniture to the acetate sides using Southern Pride parts and then glued them on.

The roof edges were then extended to cover the top of the new sides using plastic strip carefully glued to the roof and blended in with sanding sticks. The slightly weedy Lima roof vents were filed off and holes drilled to accept new castings that went in the same place. The ends needed little modification, just some additional handrails, while the buffers were replaced with large ferry ovals from S-Kits, which are not quite correct but pretty close. On the real GUVs, they were small round-headed buffers with a larger 'chopped round' head welded over the top.

The underframe layout of the Ferry GUVs was slightly different to the regular ones in order to accommodate the dual brake equipment and some ferry fittings. All of the brake gear came from the spares box, mostly Southern Pride etched parts for the V-hangers and cranks and S-Kits castings for the cylinders and tanks, along with Parkside vacuum cylinders.

Finding quality photos of these vans is hard but I was lucky enough to have a friend of a friend who could get access to the two vans parked at Eastleigh, which have since moved to the Mid-Hants Railway. The photographs were invaluable in helping to position the brake gear, equipment cabinets (a couple are scratchbuilt, most are the original parts repositioned), ferry tie-downs (from a 51L etch) and end pipework. The ETH gear was a combination of Hornby Class 50 spares and scratchbuilt parts. Replica Railways BR1 bogies were fitted in place of the Lima originals by opening out the hole in the floor with files and curved blades as well as thinning the floor until the bogies clipped in with a little bit of play.

I renumbered the van with Railtec numbers, patch painting the old number out. Additional markings came from a Cambridge Custom Transfers sheet specifically for the ferry vans. After a coat of varnish to protect the acetate, I weathered the van using enamel-based washes to tone down the bright but accurate freight brown finish.

Ferry CCT

Following some discussions about the GUV, I was sent some silhouette-cut sides for another and the shorter CCT by fellow DEMU member Alan Monk. The slab sides lend themselves to this style of production and so buoyed by the seeming ease of construction of the first, I embarked on a batch build of four more vehicles, three CCTs and one GUV.

The GUV was easier than the first, the thinner sides requiring less hard work with the file on another donor body and the underframe coming together in record time, as I had already done it once. The CCTs were a different matter altogether! Based on a shortened Lima CCT body, in hindsight it would have been easier to use the spare end castings I had to scratchbuild a new van completely.

Having successfully glued the thin sides to the Lima bodyshell, minor disaster struck as

ABOVE: The catalyst for the whole project, the Mopok sides reconditioned and fitted to a Lima GUV. ADB889201 still retains its original livery and its considerable amount of lettering but is now in departmental use.

Stores on the move

I attempted to fit the end door hinges and chalk boards, resulting in some unsightly sink marks in the sides where the solvent attacked the plastic, even though the underlying bodyshell was solid. Even after several rounds with filler and a gap-filling undercoat, sink marks are visible in the bodysides.

The underframe component list is almost identical to the GUV and the unique brake arrangement requires at least ten V-hangers within the 20ft wheelbase. I purchased a Mainly Trains etch from 51L for the inner ones and employed Southern Pride examples just for the outside ones. The underframe is built on a false floor made from 40-thou sheet that fits in to the underside of the Lima moulding. The underframe sides, ends and fillet details are made from plastic strip of various sizes. The springs and axleboxes are resin castings (again by Alan) of the W-irons from the Kitmaster/Airfix/Dapol Interfrigo van, carefully filed down to the springs and hangers and glued to MJT heavy duty compensated W-irons. The suspension details were completed with plastic strip cut and filed to shape and superglued on, with Southern Pride stepboard etches and Archer rivet transfers for the W-iron bolts. Buffers were the round-headed ferry type by Lanarkshire Models and Supplies.

The Lima CCT roof had to be shortened from the middle to retain the lip that fitted securely over the ends, with the vents filed flat and then drilled to accept new cast ones. The spacing is the same as on the GUV in a staggered pattern. On one van, I fitted just the stump of a vent as the real van ran for over a decade with just the pipe part of the vent sticking out of the roof.

The second GUV was painted in olive green as was one of the CCTs. The other two were finished with various shades of freight brown and maroon to represent the patchy nature of these vehicles in the 1980s. Decals are a mix of Cambridge Custom Transfers, Railtec, Woodhead and Replica along with, on one CCT, hand-painted yellow elephant silhouettes. These were applied to a number of vehicles in the Southern Region Power Supply Section fleet. Weathering was applied with various enamel washes, including a very thin Tamiya wash marketed as a panel liner, followed by a coat of matt varnish.

ABOVE: The ferry CCTs again use sides produced by a silhouette cutter mated with a shortened Lima CCT. Many of these vehicles retained bauxite after transfer to M&EE use, as demonstrated by a partially touched-up DB889019.

LEFT: The external condition of these vehicles was sometimes a patchwork quilt with ADB889016 having seen olive panels applied to cover up the old lettering and new details applied over the top. Building the new underframe on these vans is complex with new suspension and brake gear required.

ABOVE: Although transferred to M&EE use, repainted in olive green and given Rolling Stock Engineers (RSE) branding, ADB889010 was still clinging to its previous and now incorrect RBX TOPS code, this denoting a runner wagon.

Modelling BR Departmental Coaching Stock 71

Stores on the move

Crewe stationery stores

ABOVE: A fleet of 15 LMS-design 50ft Full Brakes were allocated to the stationery stores traffic, handling the bulk distribution runs across the country and travelling via parcels services. These had already seen their gangway connections removed and apertures plated up prior to transferring to the traffic. On March 15, 1982, XDB977030 was recorded at York Carriage Sidings, these vehicles seeing an exceptionally rare use of the X prefix, this denoting stores department vehicles. The additional lettering on the bodysides gives the Pool 5083 allocation, again quite unusual to see on a coach, along with instructions to return the vehicle to the stationery stores at Crewe. Simon Bendall Collection

Until the late 1980s, most ancillary railway equipment was transported by train and the departmental wagon fleet still included a number of increasingly elderly vans eking out their final years carrying a wide range of items. Amongst these were the various documents, forms, timetables, and other printed materials which BR staff required, and much of this was stored until needed at the British Railway Board's Paper & Printing Stationery Stores at Crewe. The stores were situated a short distance north of Crewe station, near to the BREL Works, with a dedicated pool of vehicles including both bogie and two-axle vans being allocated to convey the stationery traffic.

In November 1982, this pool (No. 5083) comprised 15 former LMS 50ft Full Brakes (BG), all recoded QRV, along with a selection of 12 two-axle vans. These included six BR fish vans, five of which had been recoded ZRW while the sixth, having been renumbered, was coded as a QRV. There were also six 12-ton ZRVs in the pool; two being LMS-design but BR-built Vanfits to diagram 1/200, two LMS-design and BR-built fruit vans to diagram 1/230, and two LMS-design LNER Vanfits to diagram 195.

At the Stationery Stores, items for a particular location would be selected and loaded into large, numbered baskets, these then being tripped the short distance to Crewe station in the two-axle vans where the baskets would be transferred, either to a parcels train or into the guard's compartment of a passenger working. All the two-axle vans were lettered to work between Crewe Stationery Stores and Crewe station and, until the mid-1980s, a visit would usually find two or three of them standing in one of the south-end bay platforms.

For multiple consignments, which would be despatched to other regional centres, the bogie Full Brakes were used, these all being built to diagram 2171. These would normally be attached to a parcels train in Crewe station so, for example, on November 16, 1982, the BGs were en route to Brighton, Bristol, Cardiff, Manchester Mayfield, Newcastle, Wimbledon, and York.

There was also a regular movement of printed material from Crewe Stationery Stores to Bricklayers Arms depot at Bermondsey. Opened as a passenger station by the South Eastern Railway in 1844, Bricklayers Arms had soon been converted into a goods depot and by the 1970s was

RIGHT: Until 1983, the Crewe Stationery Stores pool included five air-piped former insulated fish vans numbered XDE87769, 87813/14/93 and 88043, along with one that had been renumbered as XDB975957 but had not been air-piped. ZRW XDE87813 is pictured in one of the bay platforms at Crewe station in March 1981 and still in its original white livery beneath the grime. Th 'blue spot' symbol is also just discernible above the number panel. David Ratcliffe

Stores on the move

also an important destination for parcels traffic. The loads for Bricklayers Arms were often carried in 12-ton Vanfits and Vanwides drawn from the general nationwide van pool, with these being routed via Crewe Basford Hall Yard and the wagonload freight network.

By 1985, three BR diagram 1/217 Vanwides had been added to pool 5083 in the form of XDB782915, XDB783743 and XDB783889 but all the LMS BGs and fish vans had been withdrawn. The remaining vehicles were thereafter confined to working between the stores and Crewe station until the traffic ended in the late 1980s.

LEFT: The pool of vans retained until the late 1980s to carry printed materials from the stationery stores the short distance to Crewe station included various vans of LMS design. Built to diagram 1/200 at Wolverton in 1949, 12-ton plywood-bodied sliding-door van XDB751061 is seen awaiting unloading at Crewe station in August 1981. This is branded 'To work between Crewe station and Crewe Stationery Stores'. At the station, the wicker hampers of printed material would be transferred to parcels and passenger trains for distribution around the country. David Ratcliffe

ABOVE LEFT AND ABOVE RIGHT: Recorded in platform 2 at Crewe station during January 1985 were XDB750577 and XDB875188. Although BR built, both ZRVs display their LMS design influence with the former being a standard fitted van and the latter a former fruit van, as evidenced by the ventilators along the lower body. Both again have the local restriction lettering seen on their sister van, albeit with a subtle difference in the case of the fruit van which is 'To run between' rather than 'To work between'. David Ratcliffe

ABOVE: Another of the LMS BGs is recorded at York but this time within the station as XDB977023 resides in a bay platform on September 26, 1981, coupled to a Mk.1 GUV. The extended use of these vans allowed four to survive into preservation while most of the others were scrapped in 1986/87. Four found further use at Wembley depot as stores vans, allowing them to linger into 1991/92 before disposal. Simon Bendall Collection

Pool 5083 Printed Material Crewe Stationery Stores to various. November 16, 1982

Number	TOPS	Type
XDB750577	ZRV	12-ton LMS-design BR built Vanfit, diagram 1/200
XDB751061	ZRV	12-ton LMS-design BR built Vanfit, diagram 1/200
XDB875188	ZRV	12-ton LMS-design BR built Fruit Van, diagram 1/230
XDB875399	ZRV	12-ton LMS-design BR built Fruit Van, diagram 1/230
XDE283799	ZRV	12-ton LMS-design LNER Van, diagram 195
XDE298165	ZRV	12-ton LMS-design LNER Van, diagram 195
XDB87769	ZRW	BR Insulated Fish Van
XDB87813	ZRW	BR Insulated Fish Van
XDB87814	ZRW	BR Insulated Fish Van
XDB87893	ZRW	BR Insulated Fish Van
XDB88043	ZRW	BR Insulated Fish Van
XDB975957	QRV	BR Insulated Fish Van (previously E87948)
XDB977023	QRV	LMS 50ft Full Brake (previously M31420M)
XDB977024	QRV	LMS 50ft Full Brake (previously M31402M)
XDB977025	QRV	LMS 50ft Full Brake (previously M31393M)
XDB977026	QRV	LMS 50ft Full Brake (previously M31388M)
XDB977027	QRV	LMS 50ft Full Brake (previously M31409M)
XDB977028	QRV	LMS 50ft Full Brake (previously M31401M)
XDB977029	QRV	LMS 50ft Full Brake (previously M31403M)
XDB977030	QRV	LMS 50ft Full Brake (previously M31368M)
XDB977031	QRV	LMS 50ft Full Brake (previously M31361M)
XDB977032	QRV	LMS 50ft Full Brake (previously M31384M)
XDB977033	QRV	LMS 50ft Full Brake (previously M31351M)
XDB977034	QRV	LMS 50ft Full Brake (previously M31387M)
XDB977035	QRV	LMS 50ft Full Brake (previously M31358M)
XDB977036	QRV	LMS 50ft Full Brake (previously M31397M)
XDB977037	QRV	LMS 50ft Full Brake (previously M31407M)

Inspecting the tunnels

In typical weather for the line, 31168 heads through Garsdale in July 1985, en route from the Civil Engineers' base at Carnforth to conduct inspection or maintenance work in one of the tunnels on the northern portion of the Settle & Carlisle. The first four vehicles in the train are vacuum-braked Grampus wagons, the leading pair modified with work platforms while the others carry large items of equipment, including a compressor. The Southern-design Vanfit bringing up the rear, almost certainly DB753018, will be carrying lighting equipment, tools and possibly also bags of cement to the worksite. *Trevor Mann Collection*

Inspecting the tunnels

The care and upkeep of the many tunnels on the BR network posed particular challenges for the Civil Engineers. In this section, Trevor Mann examines the many specialist vehicles used in the inspection and maintenance of these structures.

During what has come to be known as the 'traditional' period, the routine inspection of tunnels was the responsibility of local teams of gangers, who walked their stretch of line two or three times each week, checking the safety of the line and correcting minor faults like displaced keys or loose fishplate bolts.

Given the danger of being struck by passing trains, the already poor visibility made worse by smoke from locomotives, the hazardous underfoot conditions and water running from the roof, walking any tunnels on their patch must have been something of a nightmare! Nevertheless, while their primary concern was the permanent way, they would also have been looking for any falls of rock, peeling brickwork or other problems with the structure itself.

Problems reported by staff on the ground were followed-up by a detailed inspection by the District Engineer, or by a suitably qualified and experienced member of his team. Such inspections were, in any case, conducted at least every two years, rather more frequently in tunnels where difficulties had been experienced previously, and involved vehicles specially equipped with a high-level platform to give access to the arch and crown of the tunnel.

Although the Southern Region adopted a rather more sophisticated solution, the vast majority of tunnel inspection vehicles were just converted open wagons. Some had been built as civil engineers' ballast wagons, but others were 'medium' or 'high' goods wagons, redundant in revenue traffic and transferred into departmental use. Their conversion consisted of erecting a sturdy framework inside the bodywork, this being topped-off with a flat work platform. Bogie vehicles were less commonly used, probably because suitable donor vehicles were rarely available for modification, but examples of Salmon, Sturgeon and Dolphin all existed.

ABOVE: Already some 40 years old when photographed at Ardrossan in August, 1981, ex-LNER 40-ton Dolphin rail and sleeper wagon DE773112 was one of relatively few bogie wagons modified for tunnel maintenance work. Its greater length allowed a more spacious work platform, safely accessed by steps, while the area beneath was available for large items of equipment like compressors or pumps. A lockable cabin at the far end provided storage for tools and materials, while the open storage area at the near end was occupied by loose equipment including a tank and timber trestles. It was accompanied by DM707106, an ex-LMS beer tank, to supply water, and with staff accommodation provided by heavily-modified brake van DM731000, the wagon had recently seen use in tunnel grouting operations. *Trevor Mann*

74 www.keymodelworld.com

Inspecting the tunnels

RIGHT: Some of the most common tunnel inspection vehicles were those converted from ballast wagons built for the Civil Engineers. The modification was comparatively straightforward, consisting of a sturdy framework supporting a flat high-level platform giving access to the upper arch and crown of the tunnel. Nevertheless, as they were the product of local workshops, there were numerous design variants. This is BR-built Tunny DB991083 at Radyr in April 1984, which had a complex framework built up from steel angle. It is joined by DW150169, a GWR Bloater assigned to the Pooley weighing machine contractors. *Trevor Mann*

Vans as well

Covered vehicles, primarily vans and cattle wagons redundant in revenue-earning use, were also converted for tunnel inspection and maintenance work, the arced roof being removed and replaced by a flat platform while the interior became available for storage of materials and equipment. Brake vans and passenger coaches were also converted, with their interiors sometimes used for staff accommodation, but these were few and far between.

More specialist vehicles were also used in tunnel maintenance work as the decades progressed and equipment improved. These included tunnel ventilation units, which featured an industrial strength fan and diesel generator fixed to a suitable wagon to draw air through the tunnel while work was in progress to reduce temperatures and clear dust. Tank wagons were used to provide water for mixing cement and grout; some were purchased second-hand, but others consisted of a smaller tank mounted onto a rail underframe.

With most of the tunnels on Britain's rail network now over 150 years old, it is testament to their design and construction, and to their subsequent inspection and maintenance, that so few accidents have resulted from faults in these structures. The most recent such occurrence, unconnected to any ongoing major reconstruction work, appears to have been the collapse of 'Black Harry' Tunnel on an obscure freight-only branch to the north of Manchester in April 1953, almost 70 years ago.

Indeed, the December 1984 fire in Summit Tunnel, which followed the derailment of a train of motor spirit and itself the result of a rolling stock defect rather than any fault in the tunnel, spectacularly demonstrated the strength of such structures. Despite being subjected to intense heat, with temperatures rising to over 1500°C at the height of the fire, the structural integrity of the tunnel was not compromised, and it was returned to use within eight months following surprisingly minor repair work. The boast of its engineer, George Stephenson, made some 140 years earlier at the time of its opening, "I stake my reputation and my head that the tunnel will never fail so as to injure any human life" had been vindicated in a manner that he could never have imagined!

ABOVE: In contrast, unfitted Grampus DB986706 had its frame constructed from timber baulks when captured at Hunslet Yard, Leeds, on May 20, 1989. The short, vertical lengths of tube, highlighted in white, along the side of the deck are thought to be locating points for plug-in lights. The two modified Grampus which appear in the Garsdale photo also have frameworks of timber construction but of a noticeably different design. *Trevor Mann*

ABOVE: Photographed at Radyr Yard on May 28, 1985, vacuum-braked Grampus DB991598 featured a framework made of steel that is clearly simpler than that on the Tunny above. Brandings include 'Pool No. 8606' and the CO symbol, this being a hangover from GWR practice and standing for 'Construction Only', as in engineers' traffic. *Trevor Mann*

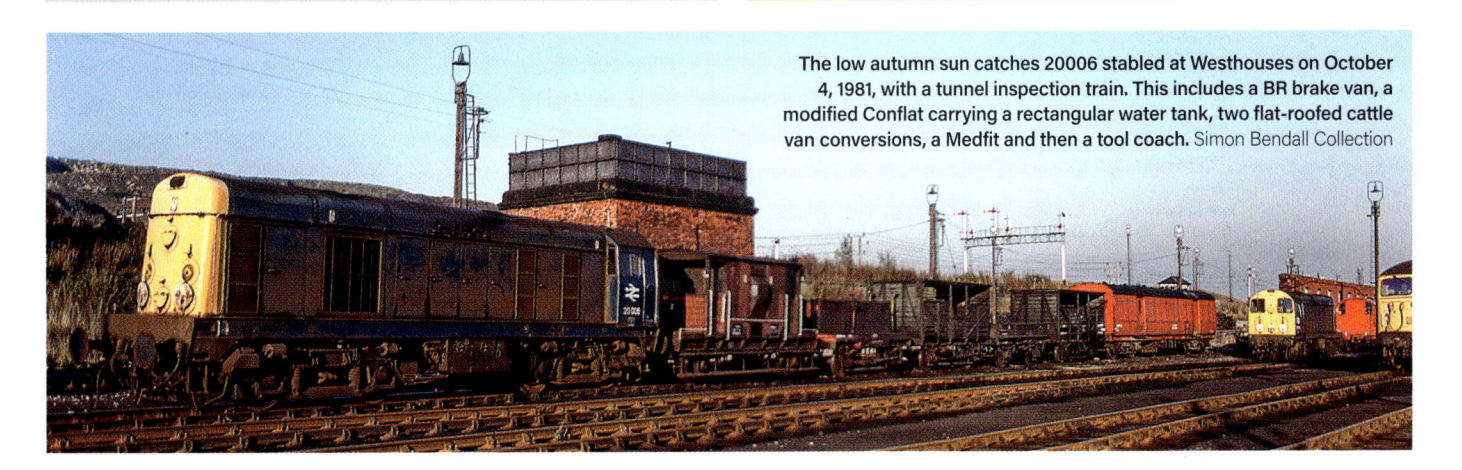

The low autumn sun catches 20006 stabled at Westhouses on October 4, 1981, with a tunnel inspection train. This includes a BR brake van, a modified Conflat carrying a rectangular water tank, two flat-roofed cattle van conversions, a Medfit and then a tool coach. *Simon Bendall Collection*

Modelling BR Departmental Coaching Stock 75

Inspecting the tunnels

Tunnel inspection wagons

ABOVE: Tunnel inspection wagons based on five-plank goods wagons were rather less common than modified Medfits, and conversions of the shock-absorbing variant were even more unusual. Pictured after withdrawal at York Leeman Road permanent way depot on May 29, 1984, the low sun highlights the distinctive Southern-design vacuum brake used on DB720747. Its inspection platform was supported by a simple wooden framework. The lettering reveals that it had once been allocated to Leyton depot in East London but had subsequently seen use in the tunnels on the southern section of the East Coast Main Line. Trevor Mann

ABOVE: Although less numerous than the opens considered up to this point, goods vans offered an alternative route for modification to tunnel inspection vehicles and had the advantage that the interior became available for secure stowage of tools, small equipment, and materials. Again, the adaptation was relatively straightforward and was just a matter of removing the original arced roof, cutting down the ends and fitting a platform level with the top of the sides. Illustrated at Burton upon Trent on April 21, 1979, black-liveried DE261019 was a modified ex-LNER van built during World War Two with match-boarded bodywork. The LMS Medfit to the right is carrying the components of a scaffolding gantry and a spotlight while the BR Medfit on the other side has the ubiquitous compressor and a fuel drum. Simon Bendall Collection

ABOVE LEFT AND ABOVE RIGHT: The withdrawal of BR from the movement of livestock traffic during the 1960s released a fleet of vacuum-braked wagons that could be relatively easily modified for tunnel inspection and maintenance. Two of these re-purposed cattle vans were recorded at Healey Mills on February 22, 1987, with DB891364 being a converted Southern-design but BR-built example. Its partner was DB891054, a similarly modified van of LMS design. Trevor Mann

BELOW LEFT: Numbered in the rarely seen DB976xxx series and recorded at Ditton sleeper depot on December 29, 1988, DB976053 was one of four LNER-design fruit vans rebuilt for service in the tunnels of the Merseyrail system. In addition to their flat high-level work platforms, these vans were equipped with steps and end-doors to allow staff to move between the vehicles without descending to track level. Retractable safety rails and adjustable floodlights are clearly visible on the platform. Rather curiously, although DB976053 and DB976054 were also converted to air brakes, DB976055 and DB976056 retained their original vacuum brakes. Trevor Mann

BELOW RIGHT: The BR standard design of cattle wagon, which was based on GWR practice, is depicted by DB893618 at Burton upon Trent on April 21, 1979. This later modification is subtly different in that the platform overhangs the sides and ends but the most noticeable aspect is undoubtedly the livery as this van has been repainted in engineers' olive green instead of the bright lime green of the earlier pair. The Medfit to the left is clearly loaded with lighting equipment while the wagon on the right is a Conflat A fitted with a rectangular tank to supply water. Simon Bendall Collection

Inspecting the tunnels

Manchester's tunnel trains

DM395378 looks good in yellow at Dewsnap Sidings on April 17, 1981. Despite the vehicle being 57 years old at this point, it would last in BR stock for another decade, being scrapped on site at Newton Heath in December 1991. Trevor Mann

When it was observed in Dewsnap Sidings in April 1981, this Manchester Division tunnel inspection train was formed of four modified ex-LMS Medfit wagons and accompanied by a staff coach converted from an ex-LMS passenger vehicle. Taking the latter first, DM395378 was simply lettered 'Riding Van', having been built at Derby Works in 1924 as a LMS Third Open before moving to the departmental fleet in 1959 as a staff coach.

Three of the accompanying Medfits were fitted with full-length, high-level work platforms supported by a fairly simple wooden framework but, unusually, these were extended by hinged boards spanning the gap between adjacent wagons. Kickboards also ran along each side of the platform and there were safely rails in their retracted position, which were lifted and secured in place on site. Additional rails were also fitted outside the framework, ensuring the safety of staff working at the lower level.

The fourth of the Medfits was DM479533. Originally the same as the other three, this had recently had its platform and support framework cut back to provide space for a set of steps instead of the more typical ladder, this providing safe access to the train's high-level working area.

LEFT: The newness of the alterations made to DM479533 can be gauged by the freshness of the wood. Steps of this nature were not commonly seen but would certainly have made getting equipment and materials onto the high platform easier. The central part of the end-planking had also been removed, a step fitted, and a handrail provided to allow staff to transfer across from the staff coach easily. Trevor Mann

ABOVE: Ex-LMS Medium Goods DM479106 displays its work platform, the hinged bridging pieces between wagons being slightly unusual. Adjustable floodlights were also fitted with the junction box located inside the supporting frame at the nearest end. DM479446 and DM479478 were modified in identical fashion. Trevor Mann

ABOVE: Four years after the Medfits and coach were photographed, 31240 coasts through Manchester Victoria in June 1985 returning to Guide Bridge permanent way depot, in all probability from the troublesome Farnworth Tunnels on the line to Bolton. Its train consists of seven vacuum-braked Grampus, two of which have been fitted with high-level platforms although, in contrast to those illustrated above, these are lightweight structures constructed from standard scaffolding components. By this date, the workforce was often transported to sites by road, hence the lack of staff accommodation in this train. Simon Bendall Collection

Modelling BR Departmental Coaching Stock 77

Inspecting the tunnels

A Manchester tunnel train by Bob Taylor

ABOVE: The converted cattle wagon uses the Dapol kit and helps mark the tunnel inspection train out as something different at exhibitions with its distinctive flat roof.

Seeking something a little different to run on the Manchester Model Railway Society's OO gauge Dewsbury Midland layout, it was decided to put together a tunnel inspection train based on the formations typically seen in the region during the BR corporate era. This was not based on a specific set of vehicles but a generic formation that included all the key vehicles required.

The first vehicle to be tackled was the distinctive flat-roof conversion of a cattle van, this using the Dapol/Airfix kit as a starting point as it represented the closest match to the real wagon, a diagram 1/353 BR-built vehicle. The advantage of the later Dapol version of the kit is the inclusion of metal wheels instead of the plastic ones in the original Airfix version. The real wagon appears to have been converted for the Nottingham area Civil Engineers division.

The building was straightforward, the main structural change being to square off the ends and add some bracing across the width, either side of the door gaps. The underframe was built as per the instructions except I substituted cast spindle buffers from Lanarkshire Models and Supplies. The ends were squared-off with a razor saw and cleaned up, regularly checking the height against the side panels. At this point, I decided the overscale plastic representing the bars on the wagon sides needed to come off. I drilled holes in the end uprights and threaded wire through as a replacement. Once this was done, I fixed the six panels to the frame, cut a pair of square micro-rod braces to the right width, and glued them across the wagon either side of the door gap.

The three-piece doors needed quite a bit of trimming to get a good fit, with most of the overscale hinges being removed and everything glued-up solid. I next cut four lengths of 'L'-shaped girder strips for the sides and ends, trimmed the corners to a rough 45 degree angle and attached them along the top edge of the wagon to form the basis for the platform. At this point, the interior was given a coat of dirty brown and weight added in the form of a couple of steel washers. Once dry, micro-rod planking strips were cut and individually glued across to form the roof platform.

The underframe was painted a mixture of black and brown using Lifecolor acrylics. The body was given a couple of coats, a red oxide shade then a wash of dirty black/brown. Once dry, a dusting of weathering powders followed, this being a mixture of black and brown. I worked this into the corners and around the frame, the finishing touch being a few dry brushed strokes of white and a hint of black. I used artist oils for this, squeezing the paint onto a scrap of card to draw out the oil with a few downward streaks to represent dribbled cement.

Grampus conversion

My choice for the Grampus fitted with the inspection platform was the Dapol vacuum-fitted version but the unfitted examples were

BELOW: The other key vehicle of the train is the Grampus equipped with the inspection platform, this being something that is rarely seen modelled.

Inspecting the tunnels

also used while Parkside provides a suitable alternative for those who want to go down the kit route. The upright supports for the inspection platform were cut from thick plastic strip and the cross bracing added; Paul Bartlett's photo site has quite a few examples illustrated, and they all differ.

Two lengths of 'T' section were then used to support the platform planking with 'L' section for the end supports. At this point, I added some interior detail such as barrels, cement sacks and a 3D-printed portable generator. The wagon had already been part-weathered previously, so I painted the new framing and touched over the weathered interior and contents. For the framing, it was just a coat of mid grey and then a wash of colour mixed to look like watery cement was used on the interior.

The planks for the deck are individually cut again and glued in place followed by a wash of grey. The detailed weathering was done on this wagon with artist oils with the paint again put on a piece of card to draw the oil out. Three colours are really all I used here, white, lamp black and burnt umber. White with a touch of burnt umber was dry brushed downwards; there is almost no visible paint needed on the brush to represent dribbles and spills.

Other wagons

The other open wagons employed in the train were another Dapol Grampus, two Bachmann 12-ton Pipe wagons and a LMS medium open. Again, these were not based on specific examples, just selected to give the correct overall impression. The main task for these was to load and weather them appropriately so a pair of 3D-printed cement mixers from eBay provided a load for two of the wagons, with pallets and sacks added alongside. Some received the upright posts in the corners that were used as supports for a daisy chain of lights when working in the tunnels.

The Medfit was used for the bowser wagon, again based on a photograph I found on the internet. I cannot recall the exact source for the bowser, but it came as a kit via a German supplier of military vehicles. Blue cotton thread was used to represent the rope lashing it down while the compressor came from Kernow Model Rail Centre and was tied down using a picture of the real thing as reference; the small wooden batons used to stop the rope fraying on the edges of the compressor came from coffee stirrers.

A general coating of dirty black was washed over the olive green of the Pipe wagon containing the compressor with a few planks picked out using oils. A mix of burnt umber with a hint of black was then dry brushed over the underframes of all the wagons to bring out the detail. Finally, an ex-LMS 12-ton van was added to the train as a stores van. This required the least work, just adding the 'Stores' lettering to the door on a blank-painted plank. This is a straight copy of the stores van used in the Huddersfield area tunnel train, again good pictures can be found on the Flickr photo website.

The mess coach is based on one of the olive drab liveried Hornby Mk.1s in its current range, this first being dismantled, and the interior given a coat of brown paint to tone down the plastic finish. Some of the windows then had scraps of orange carrier bag glued over them to represent the curtains, a common feature of many coaches of the time and one I have added to revenue rolling stock as well.

A wash of dirty black-brown acrylic was brushed on and then as it dried, taken off with cotton buds, the roof getting a slightly thicker coat. The faded white was a powder sparingly brushed down the sides, this works on the basic matt olive better than dry brushing. If working locally, motive power for these types of trains was sometimes a Class 08 because of the minimal exhaust emitted when idling for prolonged periods within the confines of a tunnel and this is recreated when the train runs on Dewsbury Midland.

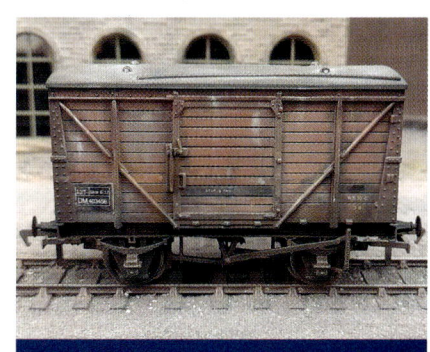

ABOVE: The Kernow air compressor is the load for the olive green Bachmann Pipe wagon with the lashing arrangement based on a photograph of the real thing.

ABOVE: Another Bachmann 12-ton Pipe, this features another cement mixer, a laser-cut ladder, and more lighting poles.

ABOVE: Also from the RTR Bachmann range is this olive green LMS Medfit containing a water bowser.

ABOVE: No tunnel inspection train is complete without a stores van, this example being realistically weathered like the rest of the set.

ABOVE: This Dapol Grampus has received a 3D-printed cement mixer as a load along with drums and sacks. A lighting pole can be seen behind the mixer.

ABOVE: Although generic in nature, the Hornby Mk.1 stands out in its weathered form and finishes off the train nicely.

Modelling BR Departmental Coaching Stock 79

Inspecting the tunnels

LEFT: Tunnel inspection gantry wagon DS2116 is seen on what may have been its very first assignment, the renewal of some brickwork on the underside of a bridge arch at Stewarts Lane around 1961. While the gantry remains in line with the underframe, the platform has clearly been extended and, because of the height of the arch, lightweight scaffolding erected on the deck. Lens of Sutton Association

The Southern's tunnel gantries

The Southern Region inherited a number of traditional tunnel inspection wagons, many converted from pre-grouping opens, and these remained in use throughout the early years of nationalisation. However, during the mid-1950s, the region adopted a novel approach to the design of such vehicles, going on to construct a number of tunnel inspection gantries which replaced most, if not all, of their elderly predecessors.

Using the illustrated DS2116 as an example, this was built at Eastleigh Works in 1960 on the underframe of one of the Southern's last 'gasholder trucks', itself constructed on the shortened underframe of a LSWR coach dating from 1904. Its superstructure consisted of a lattice steelwork gantry with timber decking on top and hinged extension supports along each side, this all being mounted on a turntable over one bogie.

Upon arrival at a worksite, the extension supports were swung out and a floor fitted, effectively doubling the width of the working surface. The turntable enabled the gantry to be swung over an adjacent track, allowing inspection of both sides and the crown of a double-track tunnel arch. A cabin for tools and materials was positioned at the opposite end to the turntable. Other examples were similar, although not all had the cabin.

Although these gantries remained useful items of equipment into the 1970s, their 70-year old wooden underframes were life-expired. While details are unclear, it appears that the underframes were condemned while the turntables and gantries from two examples were remounted onto more modern frames, thus effectively creating a pair of new vehicles. DM721211 was based on a Warwell that had seen service as a Bogie Bolster B before being transferred to the engineers' fleet and was assigned to the Bristol area for many years.

The other gantry, which remained on the Southern Region was DB975663, this being a conversion of scenery van S4593S and bore a much closer resemblance to the original vehicles. The bodywork was retained for around half the length of the vehicle, providing storage for equipment and materials, while the turntable for the gantry was mounted over the bogie at the opposite end. Both of these vehicles survived into privatisation, finally being condemned in 2000.

ABOVE: The Southern Region's tunnel inspection gantry DB975663 is seen at Ashford pre-assembly depot on March 27, 1991. Trevor Mann

ABOVE LEFT AND ABOVE RIGHT: The other tunnel inspection gantry was mounted on Warwell DM721211, which was present at Bristol East Depot on April 12, 1985. Accompanying it was Civil Engineers' staff and tool coach DS70159, this originally being a Maunsell BTK converted in 1962 and disposed of in 1998. Trevor Mann

Inspecting the tunnels

A Southern tunnel inspection unit by Paul Wade

I photographed this former Southern Railway scenery van, now numbered DB975663, several times in Ashford pre-assembly depot and also once covered for a structures technician on a night shift doing a survey with this vehicle.

After studying my photographs for the most suitable starting point, the 4mm scale Ratio Van B kit was used to provide the chassis and bogies. The Mike King scale plans for both Southern van types were used to design the body, which was formed using embossed planked plasticard with 2mm spacing. Two windows on each side were cut out with five-thou Microstrip then used to make the window frames, while the doors on each side were made using an extra layer of planked plasticard.

The bodyside ribs were formed from Microstrip, these pieces having the tops cut at a slight angle to meet the roof while they remained full width at solebar level. The single diagonal strengthening rib on each side was made in the same way with the body ends cut from 20-thou plastic sheet with the tops rounded off to match the drawings. The inner end had a doorway cut out to the left-hand side, which was framed with ten-thou strips, with one further horizontal strip between the door and the right side halfway up the end. The door was then added from behind using 20-thou Plasticard.

Further details added included three gas vents on the lower sides and one on the outer end, which were made from strip and five-thou card. On one side, the double doors were sealed shut so the plating strip down the centreline went on with both doors receiving hinge detail and the one in use the necessary door fittings. For the roof, I used the plastic moulded one from a Chivers etched scenery van kit, cutting it to the shorter length with the overhang on the inner end.

Chassis assembly

The underframe was assembled as per the instructions but minus the battery boxes and dynamo. Detail added included the handbrake wheel on each side with a plastic rod connecting them. The provided buffers were the correct type so were used as is, while the bogies were assembled with 14mm wheels and screwed to the chassis.

The body was fixed to the chassis floor with the side ribs locating over the solebars. The framework supports for the inner end of the roof were next formed from Microstrip sections, these correctly extending 3mm beyond the end of the roof. Kickboard edging strips were then added around the exposed floor section on both sides and above the bufferbeam, apart from an 18mm gap over the bogie on each side where the inspection platform pivots.

The construction of the platform began by adding two lengths of Evergreen girder section crossways on the floor. The inspection platform itself was made with a 1mm planked top 67mm long by 26mm wide. The gantry frame was many sections of Microstrip following the shapes from the photos while the solid outer end was formed from 20-thou Plasticard, which added some much-needed strength. A supporting structure for the inner end of the gantry was again made from an assortment of strip. Final detailing included adding handrail posts on the outer corners of the floor, these being 11mm tall, and 20mm ones near the centre of the floor by the access steps, these also incorporating handrails. Representations of the lights and solebar ratchet tensioners completed the job.

Once painted, the remaining windows were glazed and the roof glued on, while transfers were individual letters and numbers from Fox. The platform was fixed in position and thin blue tape run from ratchet to ratchet over the top. The last job was a light weathering of the whole vehicle.

Modelling BR Departmental Coaching Stock

Inspecting the tunnels

A somewhat work-stained 950014 stands at York Leeman Road on June 22, 1994. While it is coded YAA in the departmental series, the number prefix is incorrect, being DB instead of DC. *Mark Saunders*

Tunnel grouting train

Converted during the late-1980s and subsequently observed on several occasions in the Yorkshire area while working in Standedge Tunnel, the Eastern Region tunnel grouting train consisted of three vehicles, all equipped with air brakes. At the heart of the train was DC950014, one of the BDA bolster wagons transferred from revenue earning traffic to the departmental fleet during the early 1980s. This was modified at the Civil Engineer's Woodburn workshops in Sheffield and had a tall, part-enclosed superstructure which housed both the mixing and pumping equipment and provided a flat high-level work platform.

When seen at York in June 1994, its livery of black underframe, yellow sides and grey superstructure had by then been covered in copious deposits of grout along with graffiti. In contrast, tanker DB999099 was recorded in pristine condition at Healey Mills in May 1989. Previously numbered PR58204 and used by ICI's Mond Division in sodium hypochlorite traffic, this had been purchased secondhand to provide a water supply for the train. The final vehicle was DB786968, a heavily-modified BR ferry van. Also recorded in work-stained condition at York in June 1994, this provided mess facilities for staff working on the train.

ABOVE: **In rather better condition, ZRA water tank DB999099 was coupled to the grouting wagon at Healey Mills on May 7, 1989.** *Trevor Mann*

ABOVE: **Another extensive conversion of a 22-ton ferry van into a staff vehicle, DB786968 was residing at York on June 22, 1994.** *Mark Saunders*

82 www.keymodelworld.com

MAGAZINE SPECIALS

ESSENTIAL READING FROM KEY PUBLISHING

MODERN RAILWAYS REVIEW 2022
The railway is in the midst of significant change, as it recovers from the pandemic and begins to implement the reforms set out in the Williams-Shapps Plan for Rail.

£8.99 inc FREE P&P*

MODELLING BRITISH RAILWAYS 4 - PARCELS AND MAIL TRAINS

£8.99 inc FREE P&P*

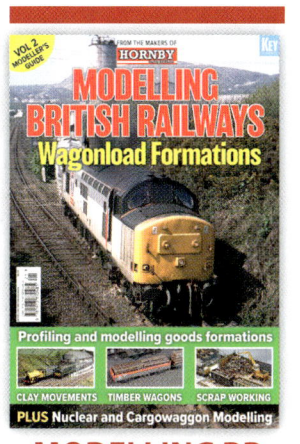

MODELLING BR WAGONLOAD FORMATIONS
The new modeller's guide.

£8.99 inc FREE P&P*

BRITISH RAILWAYS THE PRIVATISATION YEARS

£8.99 inc FREE P&P*

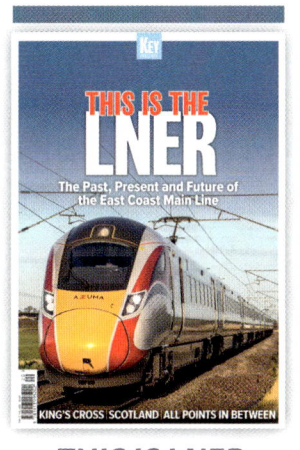

THIS IS LNER
The LNER and the East Coast Main Line -- one of the key routes linking southern England with Scotland.

£7.99 inc FREE P&P*

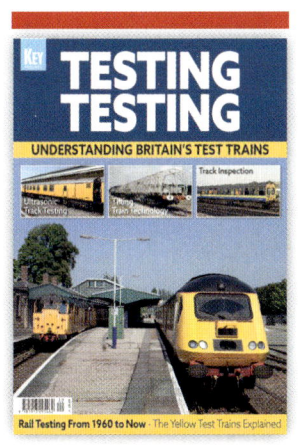

TESTING, TESTING
Understanding Britain's Test Trains.

£8.99 inc FREE P&P*

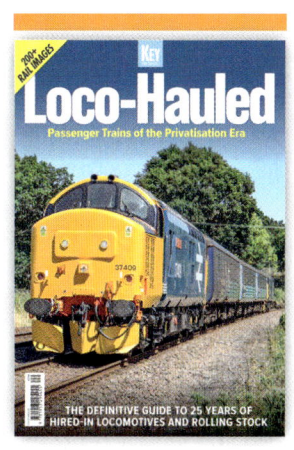

LOCO-HAULED
A must for all rail enthusiasts and modellers looking for real-life accuracy in their projects.

£7.99 inc FREE P&P*

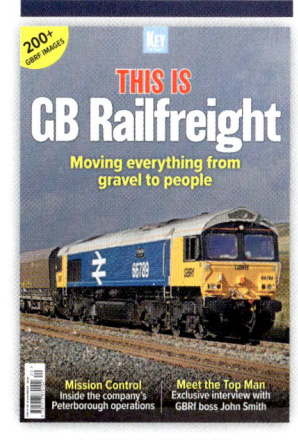

THIS IS GB RAILFREIGHT
Moving everything from gravel to people

£8.99 inc FREE P&P*

MAGAZINE SPECIALS
ESSENTIAL reading from the teams behind your **FAVOURITE** magazines

HOW TO ORDER

VISIT www.keypublishing.com/shop

OR

PHONE
UK: 01780 480404
ROW: (+44)1780 480404

*Prices correct at time of going to press. Free 2nd class P&P on all UK & BFPO orders. Overseas charges apply. Postage charges vary depending on total order value.

FREE APP
Simply download to purchase digital versions of your favourite aviation specials in one handy place! Once you have the app, you will be able to download new, out of print or archive specials for less than the cover price!

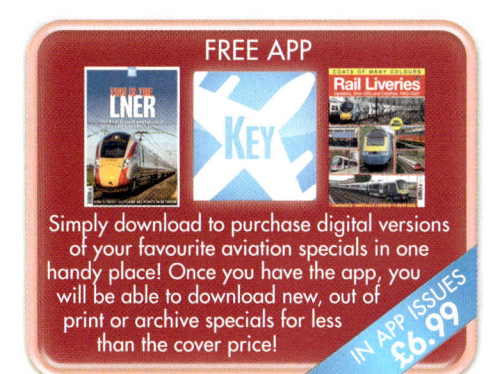

IN APP ISSUES **£6.99**

042/22

Inspecting the tunnels

Tunnel maintenance formations

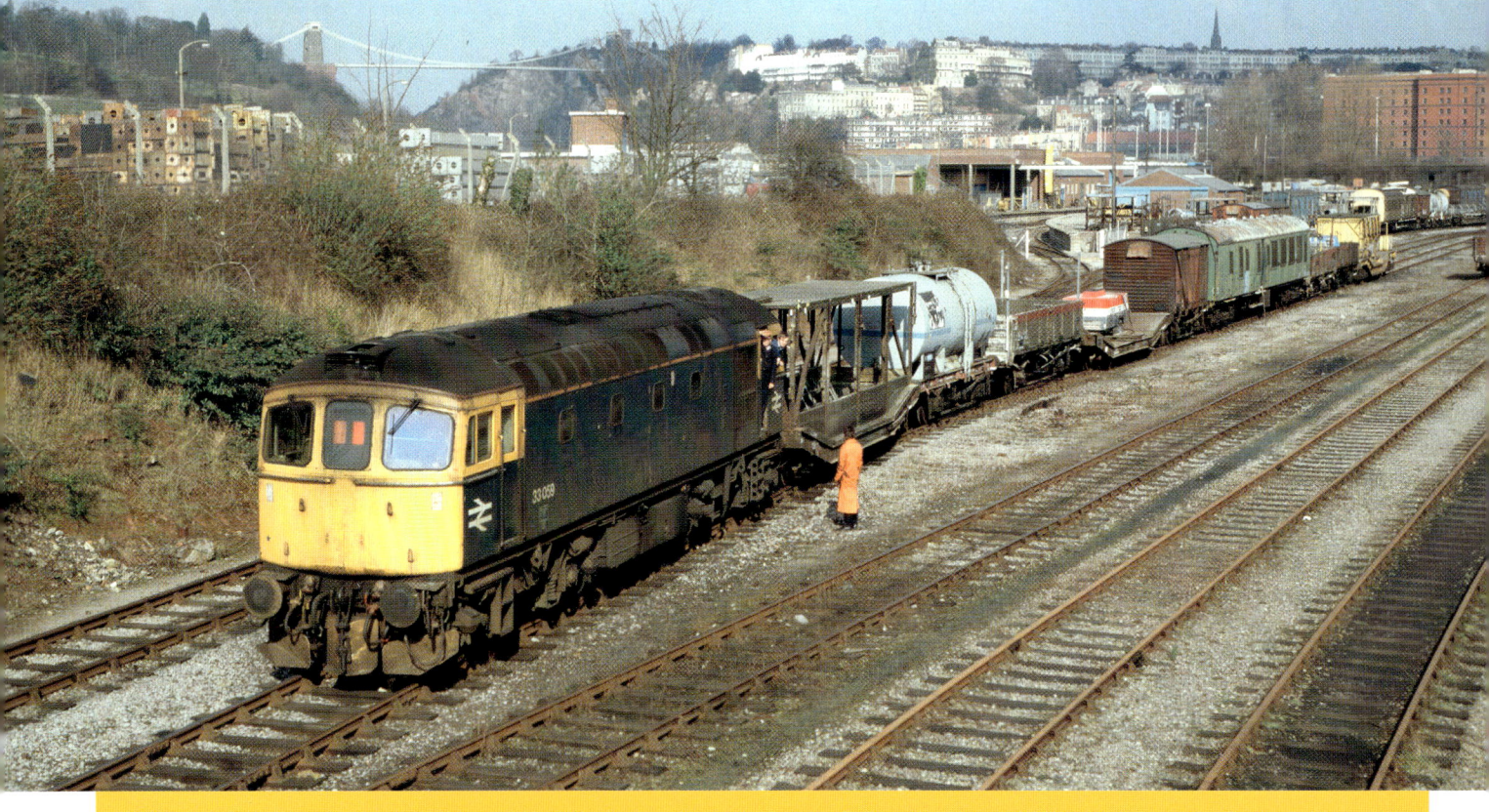

ABOVE: Set against the spectacular backdrop of the Clifton Suspension Bridge and the skyline of the city of Bristol, 33059 is seen shunting tunnel inspection and maintenance vehicles at Ashton Gate engineers' depot during the winter of 1987/88. Immediately beyond the loco is Lowmac DE230948, which has a high-level work platform and built-up sides and ends to provide space for equipment. The next vehicle is Class A tank wagon DB749658, built by Hurst Nelson for BR in 1950, which provided a water supply for grouting. This is followed by the first of three Pipe wagons, an unmodified Lowmac loaded with a hired-in compressor, and a Vanfit which, like the Pipes, conveyed equipment, and materials to the worksite. The coach is DB975058, a staff and dormitory vehicle converted from a Mk.1 BSK, while the final vehicle in the rake is DM721211, one of the tunnel gantries described on page 80. Among the vehicles in the background is DW150144, an ex-GWR Brake Third Corridor, which had been converted for tunnel inspection work; half of its roof having been replaced by a flat work platform. *Trevor Mann Collection*

RIGHT: The tunnel maintenance train operated by the Divisional Civil Engineer, Crewe was often to be found in mid and north Wales but made occasional forays further east when the tunnels on the Crewe Avoiding Lines required attention. On such an occasion in 1984, the train is seen rolling through Crewe station behind 'celebrity' Class 40 pioneer D200 (40122). Immediately behind the loco is DB996444, a 50-ton Salmon rail wagon that had been equipped with a split-level work platform supported on a steel framework sheathed in yellow-painted plywood. The second vehicle is DM731327, an ex-LMS brake van that had a work platform fitted on top of the existing arced roof, while the interior was available for the storage of tools, small items of equipment and bags of cement. As this was no longer a functioning brake vehicle, another goods brake brought up the rear. This train was the immediate predecessor of that detailed on page 86. *Simon Bendall Collection*

Inspecting the tunnels

LEFT: Taken at Ashton Gate during the early months of 1992 from a vantage point close to that of the photo opposite, this shows the new tunnel inspection train that entered service in the Bristol area during the early 1990s and which, like many of the elderly vehicles seen previously, would have principally seen use in the Severn Tunnel. Immediately behind 37133, now resplendent in Civil Engineers 'Dutch' livery, is an unidentified ZBA Rudd 20-ton ballast wagon. This would have been used to convey materials to the worksite and, occasionally, to return small amounts of spoil. *Trevor Mann Collection*

ABOVE, BELOW LEFT AND BELOW RIGHT: The remaining wagons in the new train were Freightliner container flats that, redundant in their original use, had been passed to the Civil Engineers, becoming YXAs. Anticipating 21st century practice by some years, these had each been fitted with two 30-foot modules, secured to the wagons using the existing twist-locks, which provided a spacious high-level work area with the space beneath accommodating assorted equipment. DC621489 carried a large generator set and compressors, DC621537 had a caged area to house miscellaneous loose equipment while intermediate wagon DC622938 contained grouting apparatus. All three were at East Usk Yard, Newport, on August 21, 1992. *Paul Bartlett*

Modelling BR Departmental Coaching Stock 85

Inspecting the tunnels

Last of the tunnel trains

The final tunnel inspection and maintenance train to be built along traditional lines was the one modified at Chester carriage and wagon workshops during the spring of 1995. This worked from a base at Bangor and was used in the tunnels along the North Wales Coast line, six of the seven vehicles being rebuilt SKA coil wagons, themselves conversions of SPA steel plate wagons.

RIGHT: Recoded ZDA, DC461087 was photographed at Chester wagon repair depot along with the rest of the train on April 12, 1995, soon after conversion. This wagon was equipped with a full-height work platform to give access to the crown of the tunnel and was very much of the traditional design with space on the wagon floor beneath to carry materials while the platform was built of steel girders and channel section. The handrails on both the sides and ends were extendable with the deck made from substantial timber. All photos David Ratcliffe

ABOVE: Both DC460484 and DC460606 (not illustrated) were mixed half-height and full-height platform wagons that gave access to both the crown and the arch of a tunnel, these being positioned either side of DC461087 and giving access to it. Festooned with handrails, the upper ones were again extendable while the conversion budget clearly did not run to repainting the wagons as this one still retained traces of its original Railfreight red livery on the curb rail, which has faded to the usual pink.

ABOVE: Not quite the luxury of a staff coach of old! DC460815 provided some measure of staff facilities with the addition of a Portakabin-style structure to its deck, which was surrounded on all sides by safety railings. The other vehicle not illustrated was DC460743, which retained the previous SKA side rails and flat floor but gained more safety rails. This was presumably used to carry equipment such as cement mixers, compressors, and lighting stands to and from worksites.

ABOVE: Completing the set of six SKA conversions was DC461079, which gained a water tank, its size being limited by the need to keep the wagon within specified axle loadings. This was helpfully marked 'Not for drinking'! Other aspects of the conversions included retaining the original SPA ends on all vehicles, which were repainted, while the yellow fittings sticking upwards at the nearest end were the securing latches for the railing gates, as shown lowered at the other end of the wagon.

ABOVE: The tunnel inspection train was completed by BR 22-ton ferry van DB787297, which was largely unmodified for the role, even retaining its dual brake equipment so was coded ZQX. Notably, the blue repaint did not include fresh numbers for the van as the previous lettering has just been painted around! This conveyed smaller items of equipment together with materials like bagged cement to the worksite. Today, such tunnel inspection work is carried out by road-railers and scissor lifts.

Weeding the network

The railway system has long fought a battle against weeds and other intrusive vegetation, one that today it is increasingly losing. However, throughout the BR era, several specialised weedkilling trains operated across the system, most being privately-owned. Trevor Mann **recounts the history of each operator.**

Weeds growing in and around the permanent way are more of a problem than just being unsightly. Left unchecked, their root systems disrupt the drainage of water through the ballast and encourage the accumulation of clay and silt particles which, in turn, can lead to the development of 'wet-spots' that will eventually undermine the stability of the track.

Therefore, the railways have long taken steps to keep their tracks free from weeds. Until the 1960s, this was the responsibility of local 'lengthmen' who, equipped with hoes, were tasked with removing any weeds growing in or through the ballast during early summer. Their work will have been eased when the application of chemical herbicide, sprayed from 'knapsack' units or from equipment mounted on platelayer's trolleys, was introduced in the 1930s, but weed control remained a time-consuming aspect of routine track maintenance.

Although used in the United States from around the time of World War One, it was not until the 1930s that weedkilling trains were introduced in the UK. Early experiments used converted goods wagons but the more sophisticated designs that followed saw redundant coaches, often of considerable vintage, fitted out with the spraying equipment. A string of redundant steam locomotive tenders usually carried the herbicide.

The success of these early trains, combined with a general drive towards greater efficiency and reduced costs, led to the widespread adoption of this method of weed control. By the mid-1950s, over 10,000 tons of liquid weedkiller was being applied annually, some 30,000 miles of track was being treated, and all BR regions were using weedkilling trains; some undertaking the work 'in-house' while others contracted it out to specialist companies.

Different options

Taking the Southern as the 'in-house' example, the regional civil engineers operated two weedkilling trains during the late 1950s and early 1960s. Each was formed from two ex-Southern Railway Passenger Luggage Vans, one modified as the spray van and the other providing staff accommodation. Converted locomotive tenders carried the herbicide with those marshalled in one train retaining their original bodywork while those in the other had anchor-mounted cylindrical tanks. Each formation was completed by an ex-Southern 15-ton goods brake.

ABOVE: **Picture one: The Chipman weedkiller is seen just a few weeks into its first season of operation with Hunslet Barclay Class 20 power as a still nameless 20901 leads the set past Great Cheverell and east along the Berks and Hants line on April 12, 1989, with 20904 on the rear. Heading the formation is spray van CC99014, which is busily engaged on applying the chemicals trackside as well as coating the underframes of the train. Adjacent to this is a then newly-converted Mk.1 dormitory coach CC99016, with soon to be retired CC99015 next up and then BR 20-ton ferry van DB786951, which was hired for use as a stores van and also numbered CC9017 for the duration. The green livery would remain in use until the end of the 1991 weedkilling campaign.** John Chalcraft/Rail Photoprints

Moving onto the London Midland Region, Picture two illustrates DM198822, an ex-Midland Railway six-wheeled passenger brake built at Derby Works in 1910, which had been adapted to serve in the region's 'Weedkilling Train No 2'. In this period, the Chipman Chemical Co Ltd was the major specialist contractor offering weed control

Modelling BR Departmental Coaching Stock **87**

Weeding the network

services to British Railways. Its more modern trains are detailed later but those operating during the late 1950s and early 1960s are exemplified in pictures three and four, both taken around 1965.

Having provided a little in the way of historical context, the following sections consider in greater detail the weedkilling trains operating over British Rail track during the final two decades of its existence, by which time the Eastern Region had become the sole 'in house' operator. Fisons Agrochemicals was also providing effective competition to Chipman's in offering weed-control services to the remaining regions.

LEFT: **Picture two:** London Midland spray coach DM198822, lettered 'Civil Engineer Weed Killing Train No.2' is seen at Crewe on April 29, 1963, with one of the converted tenders for carrying the herbicide behind. Colour-Rail

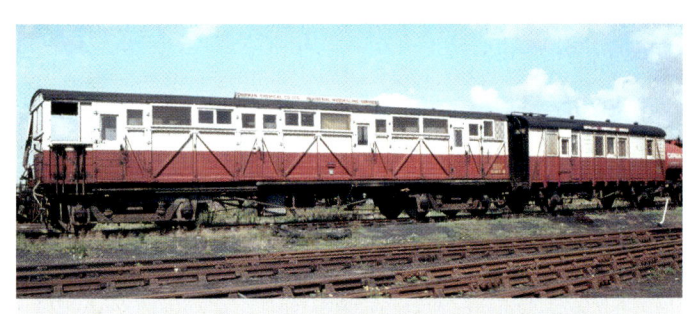

ABOVE: **Picture three:** Among the earliest Chipman vehicles was this pair, the nearer vehicle being CWT6, an ex-GWR outside-framed Siphon G modified as a spray and machinery van. Next to it is staff and dormitory van CWT2, which was a converted ex-Southern Railway Passenger Luggage Van. Trevor Mann Collection

ABOVE: **Picture four:** The furthest coach in this circa 1965 shot is either CWT9 or CWT11, both of which were ex-Southern Railway Maunsell-design Brake Composite Corridor coaches converted into spray vans. Nearer the camera is CWT4, a six-wheeled staff and dormitory van of Great Northern origin, then six of the 14-ton anchor-mounted tank wagons operated by Chipman's. These were lettered 'Chipman Chemical Company Ltd' on one side and 'Industrial Weedkilling Service' on the other and were sometimes used to make deliveries of weedkiller concentrate in addition to seeing service in the company's weedkilling trains. Peter Fidczuk Collection

ABOVE: **Picture five:** This shot of a Chipman set stabled at Wimbledon West in June 1977 provides plenty of inspiration for a yard containing both departmental stock and revenue earning vehicles, such as the empty 21-ton HTV coal hoppers on the left laying over from either Chessington or Tolworth. By their nature, Chipman sets would stable at BR depots, sidings and yards when out working with CC99009 and CC99010 being the two shown here with five tankers. Simon Bendall Collection

Weeding the network

Eastern Weedkillers

ABOVE: The Eastern Region weedkiller passes the water treatment works at Acomb Landing, on the northern outskirts of York, on June 6, 1983 in the care of 37061. Gresley spray coach DE320995 is the leading coach behind the tanks followed by stores BGs DB977016 and DB977017 and finally Mk.1 staff and dormitory coach DB975379. Simon Bendall Collection

By the mid-1970s, the Eastern Region was operating the last of BR's 'in house' weedkilling trains. Based at York Leeman Road permanent way depot, this worked over the lines of the old North Eastern Region between Yorkshire and the Scottish border.

Formed by the NER during the early 1960s, this train initially featured two ex-LNER Gresley passenger coaches, one converted to the spray coach and the other to a staff and dormitory vehicle, these being supported by four tenders recovered from withdrawn V2 steam locomotives. The original spray coach lasted only until 1963, when it was replaced by DE320995, which would survive in regular service for a further 20 years. The tenders were similarly short-lived, being superseded in 1965 by six vacuum-braked former creosote tanks, DB998966-971 having been built for British Railways in 1958.

The train ran in this form until 1974 when, reflecting a change to powdered herbicides,

ABOVE LEFT AND ABOVE RIGHT: Spray coach DE320995 is seen in York Dringhouses yard on April 24, 1983, it having been converted from a Gresley Brake Third Open 20 years earlier, which itself dated from 1935 to diagram 191. At this time, it was also numbered 88001 in the Civil Engineers Plant System (CEPS), an unusual occurrence for a coach and something more commonly found on wagons fitted with light cranes and similar equipment. The longest-surviving vehicle in the train, it would be replaced by DB977229 the following year. Trevor Mann

Modelling BR Departmental Coaching Stock **89**

Weeding the network

it became the norm to include three vans, sometimes standard BR Vanfits but more usually ex-LNER or BR fish vans, in the formation. A newly-converted Mk.1 staff and dormitory coach, DB975379, replaced the original LNER one the following year.

More Mk.1 replacements
Further changes in the formation occurred during the early-1980s when the vans were replaced by newly-converted former Mk.1 BG stores vans while the six creosote tanks were superseded by a similar number of secondhand ex-private owner tank wagons. It is in this form that the train is shown in the opening picture.

The final change in the composition of the weedkiller occurred in 1984 and saw the distinctive Gresley spray coach replaced by DB977229, another Mk1 BG (ex 80725) but rebuilt at one end with spraying equipment and observation windows. Like its predecessor, it was finished entirely in yellow.

Having served the northeast of England for a quarter of a century, albeit in a continually updated formation, the set was finally taken out of use in 1988 as part of a nationwide re-casting of weedkiller train operation that would see all such services performed by just two privately-owned air-braked trains going forward.

ABOVE: **DB977016 was one of a pair of stores vans converted from Mk.1 Full Brakes in 1981 for use in this train. It was previously 81304, built by Pressed Steel in 1957, while its partner was DB977015, this previously being 81372 and built in the same year by the same manufacturer. Sacks of the Pramatol and Atrazine herbicides used at this time are clearly visible through the windows of the loaded van. The assigned staff and dormitory coach, DB975379, is pictured in the staff coaches section on page 45.** Trevor Mann

ABOVE: **During the early 1980s, the six creosote tanks that had been part of the train since 1965 were replaced by the same number of 22-ton Class B tank wagons, these being previously owned by Texaco. Renumbered as DB999035-40, these were refurbished by WH Davis. DB999040, previously TEX47770, was pictured at Dringhouses on the same date as the other vehicles. The ring of brackets at the right-hand end of the barrel show the location of the Regent nameplates that were carried when built in 1960.** Trevor Mann

ABOVE: **Seen from the unmodified end, replacement spray coach DB977229 was recorded at York Leeman Road on June 4, 1987. It had a working life of less than five years in this form as once the Eastern Region set was withdrawn, it was scrapped at Booth's Rotherham yard in December 1988 as were the two ex BG stores vans.** Paul Bartlett

ABOVE: **In its final formation with the replacement ex BG spray coach included, 31124 traverses Colton Junction on June 23, 1984. The Shark ballast plough brake van marshalled directly behind the loco was used to assist in propelling movements when the set had to reverse at locations along its route, top and tailing by two locos being uncommon at this time.** Simon Bendall Collection

A refugee from the Southern
RIGHT: **Converted in 1960 from an ex-Southern BCK, spray van DS70070 was initially coupled to a pair of redundant locomotive tenders, and later to two tank wagons, to form a Southern Region weedkilling unit. Redundant on the Southern by 1974, it was then transferred to the Eastern Region. When photographed at its base in Skelton Sidings, York, on April 9, 1978, it was coupled to BR 22-ton creosote tank wagons DB998955 and DB998957. Painted in distinctive Southern olive drab, these are presumed to have accompanied DS70070 on its migration north, and to have worked with it on its occasional forays over Eastern Region territory. It was withdrawn in 1980 and scrapped a year later.** Paul Bartlett

Weeding the network

The Eastern weedkiller in 2mm by Tony Buckton

ABOVE: The Eastern Region BG spray coach DB977229 had an unusual look with multiple small observation windows preferred to the larger style used on the privately-owned weedkillers. The spray jets were mounted at the bottom corner of the sides and also on a bar beneath the bufferbeam.
All pictures by Tony Buckton

The catalyst for this project came in September 2016 when Revolution Trains announced its intention to produce an N gauge model of the 35t GLW Class B tank wagons, so my thoughts turned to how I could justify running them on a layout based around Hull in 1984. By this period, the type had mostly disappeared from revenue earning traffic with some being converted for departmental use as water carriers with the BR Eastern Region weedkiller train. A little research found the rest of the consist to be formed of converted Mk.1 stock and a Shark ballast plough, which were all readily available in N gauge to complete a relatively simple but interesting project.

Throughout the project, various sizes of styrene strip, card and plastic rod were glued together or to the vehicle components using Humbrol liquid polystyrene cement or the less aggressive Limonene for finer details. Brass and nickel silver components were soldered where possible or glued into drilled holes with superglue for strength and Milliput modelling clay was used for all the filling jobs. Finally, Glue-Buster from Deluxe Materials was used sparingly to assist with the disassembly of stock. Reference photos of the required vehicles were downloaded from Paul Bartlett's Zenfolio website for a very reasonable fee and were essential for the project.

Tanker alterations
The ZRV departmental water tanks had been converted from former Texaco (originally Regent) owned vehicles in the 477xx number range and sported a revised pattern of suspension. Thankfully, Revolution Trains accurately depicted this detail difference between the available models and five of the Texaco variants were sourced.

The tanks required little in the way of modification, other than a repaint, the removal of an outlet valve at one end and the addition of a fine pipe at the opposite end of the barrel. The underframe required the addition of a pair of rather prominent water feed pipes extending down from the discharge points and running beneath the length of the wagons.

The tank barrels were separated from the chassis for stripping and repainting, with the barrel ends worked out with a blunt scalpel blade and the weight removed. I stopped short of removing the etched walkways and ladders as the risk of damaging them

ABOVE: The model that started the project, Revolution Trains' Class B tankers transformed into departmental form, this being DB999039.

Weeding the network

was too great. To strip the paint, I used 99.9% Isopropyl Alcohol (IPA) with constant agitation from a glass-fibre pencil.

The aforementioned additional details were added from brass, nickel silver and plastic rod. One prominent feature of the tank barrels were the remains of the brackets that held the ownership boards in place when first built. These were represented by 0.25mm nickel silver rod glued into holes and cut off as close to the barrel as possible. An octagonal transfer was made and applied to assist with the marking and drilling of these holes. The tank barrels were airbrushed with Railmatch faded yellow enamel (reference no. 452) before re-assembly and finishing.

Spray coach

Next to be tackled was the spay coach, this being the replacement and modified Mk.1 BG DB977229 rather than the previous Gresley vehicle. The main modifications were to one end and below the solebar, so the donor Graham Farish model was reduced to its component parts and the paint stripped as above before the removal of the unwanted footsteps on the ends. One end of the body was then marked for modification; there is a correct way round as denoted by the window arrangement adjacent to the guard's door.

The sizes and positions of the additional windows and bodyside spray nozzle recesses were estimated from photos and guide transfers made to suite. These were then applied and checked before cutting began. It quickly became apparent that my original plan of cutting the recesses out individually was not going to work. I instead resorted to cutting out the complete rectangle for the six side windows and then re-building the bars between them using plastic strip glued in place.

Due to the curved sides, the bars were left proud of the surface and then filed back and profiled to match the body using progressively finer grades of wet and dry paper. The end was regularly re-primed during the process to maintain a consistent colour, as any patchy bits can create optical illusions which could result in excessive cutting or filing. Small rectangles of styrene were cut for the bodyside nozzle recesses and 0.3mm diameter plastic rod was glued along the lengths before securing them into the recesses.

The upper end windows and end door fell within the area occupied by the top moulding of the bodyshell, so this had to be cut away before they could be opened out. A replacement door and framework were fashioned from styrene and glued in place before airbrushing in the same shade of faded yellow as the water tanks. The additional windows were glazed with panels cut from clear plastic packaging and secured with Micro Kristal Clear.

Further detailing

Small detailing on the spray coach included handrails and pipe runs added to the ends along with an electrical conduit and spotlight, mostly made from 0.25mm nickel silver rod bent to shape and glued into 0.3mm diameter holes. The spotlight was created from a couple of fine strands of copper wire twisted to form a loop, the ends were then glued into a hole along with the termination of the conduit run. A blob of glue was applied to the loop to form the lamp.

Some guesswork was required regarding the position of the lamp as modifications carried out between the 1984 and 1985 seasons saw the handrails removed and the conduits re-routed to run down both outer edges of the front with a spotlight at each side. I now suspect a second lamp may have been present in the 1984 arrangement so will modify the end should evidence come to light.

Close study of photos showed that the roof had what appeared to be two large vents approximately halfway down and just off the centre line. The size of these was estimated and replicated by stacked styrene disks punched out with a leather punch and glued into position. The unwanted roof details were then sanded away, and any holes filled ready for painting. Patches of flaking paint were replicated by airbrushing in light grey enamel before creating patches with Humbrol Maskol and applying a top coat of dark grey.

The numerous underframe details were estimated from photographs and built up from various sizes of brass and nickel silver rod, scraps of brass etch and plastic. The pipework was soldered where possible with flanges and valves being replicated by wire insulation and modelling clay. Handbrake wheels and a dynamo were from the Ultima range with a grille covering the dynamo cut from a spare Class 40 frost grille. A representation of the spray bar and rubber deflector were soldered up from nickel silver 0.3mm wire and a short length of scrap fret; these were then attached in front of the spray end bogie at an estimated height and distance.

Dormitory coach

The greatest challenge in creating the dormitory coach DB975379 was making the heater flue recesses along the bodyside. I started by making and applying transfers to mark out the holes that required cutting for the recesses. After filing out, I initially tried to construct the complex internal shape from styrene strip but found it impossible to make them consistent. A solution was to create the shape in reverse onto a stamp and then use this to recreate the recesses in modelling clay. The stamp was made up from square brass tube filled at the end and then filed to as near as I could get to the correct shape. The addition of a plastic collar maintained a consistent surface around the recesses.

Once set, they were cut from the clay and glued into the holes in the bodyside. The recesses were finished with the addition of a square plate in the bottom and, in most cases, a plastic rod to represent the heater flu. Not all of the recesses retained the flu, which photographic evidence suggested varied through the life of the vehicle. One side of the coach also had the central door plated over, so this was filled and sanded back to the coach profile.

Similar to the spray coach, the gangway at one end was rebuilt to represent the framework minus the corridor connection with a window added to the door, this end going next to the loco. The body was then airbrushed with Railmatch Southern Railway

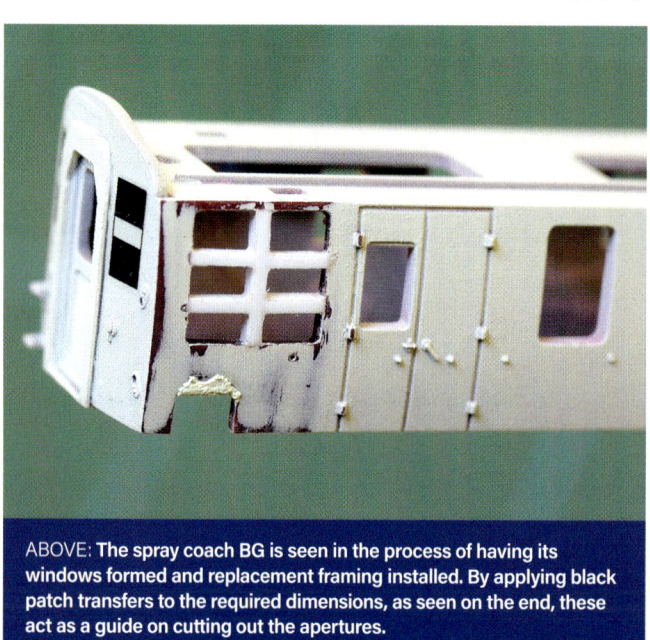

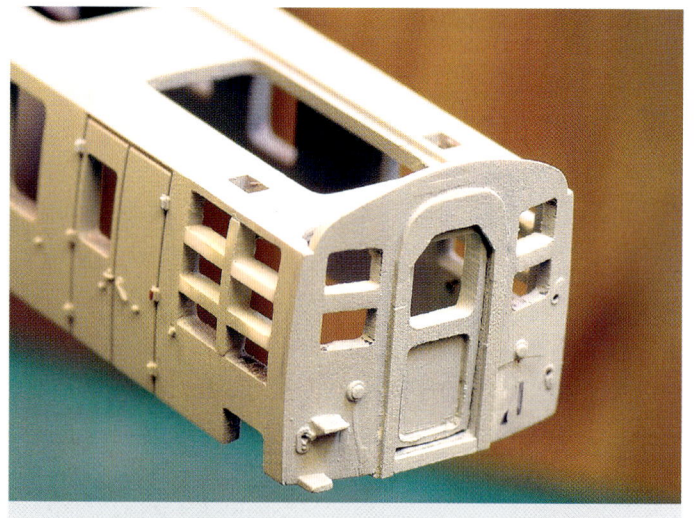

ABOVE: The spray coach BG is seen in the process of having its windows formed and replacement framing installed. By applying black patch transfers to the required dimensions, as seen on the end, these act as a guide on cutting out the apertures.

ABOVE: With the windows made in the spray coach, the remains of the corridor connection mount and modified door have been made from plastic and glued in place.

Weeding the network

ABOVE: Staff coach DB975379 requires the most home-made lettering along with gas vent recesses and a modified interior. Unlike the other coaches, this staff vehicle would survive the withdrawal of the Eastern Region weedkiller set and go on to find further work. It was eventually scrapped in 2009 after a decade or so in store at York.

ABOVE: The method used to create the vent recesses in DB975379 is shown with the stamp and modelling clay in the background with some of the dried recesses cut out and installed in the apertures in the body. One has also received the additional central flue detail.

dark olive (reference no.631) and then the doors masked and finished in faded yellow.

Unwanted roof details were cut away and the roof vents changed to a shell type (UM251) from Etched Pixels. Replacement rainstrips were added from fine styrene strip glued into place. Below the solebar, handbrake levers were added from 0.5mm brass strip soldered onto a short length of 0.25mm nickel silver rod. Whitemetal gas cylinder cabinets were added from Etched Pixels (UM240), these being reduced in height slightly before gluing in place. A small additional footstep was made from brass and added below the centre door on one side, while the solebar step was removed from the opposite side below the plated-up door.

The interior was modified by cutting back the corridor to the middle entrance and filing down the remaining seating. Some additional features were made up from styrene before painting the interior in a light grey. The ventilators on the glazing required repainting into olive green by hand before reuniting with the body, while some of the doors were modelled with replacement droplights in the open position. Orange curtains were then made from cigarette paper and positioned behind selected windows. The coach was reassembled, and pipe runs along with handrails added to the ends.

Stores vans

Little was required in the way of modifications on the two Mk.1 BG stores vans DB977015 and DB977016 other than removing the excess footsteps and modifying the handrails and filler pipes on the ends. The roof vents were also swapped to the shell type. Despite the Farish donors being olive green-liveried models, upon completing the dormitory coach in the same livery, the shades were too dissimilar so both BGs were stripped down to replace the factory finish.

To complete the project, I had to find a method of producing transfers and in particular white ones for the extensive lettering on the dormitory coach. The solution came from a German company called Ghost, which produces white toner cartridges for a large range of laser printers along with a selection of decal foils; its seven-micron blue waterslide transfer film is commendably thin.

RIGHT: The two stores vans are simple upgrades of the Farish BG with the alterations confined to removing the steam era fittings on the ends. DB977015 also shows the cosmetic improvement of replacing the factory finish with a better shade of olive green.

The transfers were all designed in black using a combination of Microsoft Word, Photoshop, and a scanned printout of lettering in the New Rail Alphabet font, as this was the closest I could find to true Rail Alphabet. The font is not an exact match but in 2mm scale, the differences are virtually indiscernible. The white transfers are printed separately by sending the job to the printer in black but with the black toner cartridge swapped with a white one from Ghost. The transfers were then applied over gloss varnish with a protective coat of satin added once dried.

From photos of the spray coach, it can be seen that it did not carry the DB977229 number and QVV TOPS code in 1984; however, what was carried cannot be made out either. I suspect that the CEPS number of 88001 featured originally and this was later covered over by a black obliteration patch when the coaching stock number was applied. As Paul Bartlett's photo clearly showed this latter arrangement, I opted to model that side as per the picture.

Finishing

General weathering was applied in a combination of thin washes, dry brushing and airbrushing using weathering colours from the Railmatch range mixed with thinners and a small amount of Humbrol Matt Cote.

A light grey colour was mixed from Humbrol matt enamels to create the herbicide overspray. This was lightly airbrushed down the stock at an acute angle in one direction, radiating away from the spray coach in a progressively lighter pattern down the train.

A variety of couplings are fitted to the coaches with the outer ends of the Mk.1s and the water tanks featuring couplings from B&B; these will couple to a simple and unobtrusive wire hook on either the train loco or the Shark ballast plough that I include in the rake, this being the N Gauge Society kit. One end of each of the Mk.1s has a wire hook designed to couple to the standard coupling on the next vehicle. This improves the coupling distances and ensures the correct orientation of the stock.

Despite an amount of guesswork and estimation being required, the project has produced a striking train and something a little out of the ordinary, which can be justified anywhere on the region in the mid-1980s.

RIGHT: Completing the weedkiller set is Shark DB993755, which was attached to assist with propelling moves. This is the N Gauge Society kit finished in dirty olive green.

Modelling BR Departmental Coaching Stock 93

Weeding the network

Chipman Weedkillers

Picture one: Chipman Chemical's 'Train 4' passes through Westbury behind a Class 33 on April 26, 1975. Finished in the company's original red and white livery, the coaches are staff and dormitory vehicle CWT8 and spray coach CWT7 behind the Crompton, later to become CC99008 and CC99007. Trevor Davis/Transport Treasury

The Chipman Chemical Co Ltd of Horsham in West Sussex was founded in 1928 as a subsidiary of the Chipman Chemical Engineering Company of the USA, which was already a leading supplier of weedkilling chemicals and contract services to American railroads. Chipman entered the UK railway weed-control business in 1932 and three years later began to supply the Southern Railway with the chemicals and spray equipment used in the company's weedkilling trains. By nationalisation in 1948, the firm had established itself as the leading supplier of weed-control chemicals, equipment, and contract services to both the main line railways and major industrial customers like the War Office.

Chipman's first post-war weedkilling train, which worked over the southern part of the Eastern Region, including East Anglia, consisted of a spray van converted from an ex-Great Eastern goods brake accompanied by four of the company's anchor-mounted tank wagons. This seems to have been short-lived as Chipman introduced a new train for use on the Eastern in 1955. Referred to as 'Train 1', this was made up of two modified ex-Southern Railway Passenger Luggage Vans. Two more trains soon followed, 'Train 2' for the North Eastern and Scottish regions in 1956 and 'Train 3' for the Western in 1958.

The former consisted of two vans of ex-Great Northern origin, both dating from before World War One, while the latter featured a modified ex-GWR Siphon and another ex-Great Northern van. All three trains included six anchor-mounted tank wagons. The photos on page 88 illustrate Chipman's trains from this period, including its tank wagons.

ABOVE: Picture two: A better look at CWT8, the future CC99008, at Westbury on April 26, 1975, shows that most of the compartments were still present but converted to dormitories, while the interior at the near end has been opened out as a mess area. Beyond the four tankers, a Southern PMV is included as a stores van. Trevor Davis/Transport Treasury

Weeding the network

Table one: Chipman vacuum-braked coaches, TOPS code PPV

Fleet No.	Tops No.	BR Diagram	Design Code	Vehicle Type
CWT7	CC99007	6/663	PP018A	Spray coach
Ex SR Maunsell four compartment BTK S3724S, built Eastleigh 1930 to SR diagram 2101.					
CWT8	CC99008	6/664	PP019A	Staff & dormitory coach
Ex SR Maunsell CK S5644S, built Eastleigh 1930 to SR diagram 2301.					
CWT9	CC99009	6/663	PP018B	Spray coach
Ex SR Maunsell six compartment BTK S6699S, built Eastleigh 1935 to SR diagram 2403. Converted in 1960 to Push-Pull Driving Brake Composite to SR diagram 2407.					
CWT10	CC99010	6/664	PP019B	Staff & dormitory coach
Ex SR Bulleid semi-open Brake Third S4035S, built Lancing/Eastleigh 1949 to SR diagram 2123.					
CWT11	CC99011	6/663	PP018B	Spray coach
Ex SR Maunsell six compartment BTK S6697S, built Eastleigh 1935 to SR diagram 2403. Converted in 1960 to Push-Pull Driving Brake Composite to SR diagram 2407.					
CWT12	CC99012	6/664	PP019B	Staff & dormitory coach
Ex SR Bulleid semi-open Brake Third S4036S, built Lancing/Eastleigh 1949 to SR diagram 2123.					
CWT13	CC99013	6/663	PP018B	Spare spray coach
Ex SR Bulleid BTK S2850S, built Lancing/Eastleigh 1945 to SR diagram 2121.					
n/a	CC99014	n/a	PP027A	Spray van, TOPS code later PPA/KCA
Ex SR scenery van S4600S, built Lancing 1949 to SR diagram 3182.					
n/a	CC99015	n/a	PP027B	Staff & dormitory van, TOPS code later PPA/KCA
Ex SR scenery van S4589S, built Ashford/Eastleigh 1938 to SR diagram 3182, subsequently adapted to carry elephants.					

Second phase

The spray and staff and dormitory coaches included in Trains 1 to 3 were withdrawn from service during the mid-1960s, being superseded by a new fleet of bogie vehicles, as detailed in table one, which would mostly survive into the 1980s.

The initial stage of this process saw the formation in 1963 of 'Train 4', this featuring in the two photos taken at Westbury in 1974 (pictures one and two). Chipman's CWT8, the staff and dormitory coach in this train, would be allocated TOPS number CC99008 and this would remain in use until the demise of Chipman's vacuum-braked trains in 1988. Later renumbered as CC99007, spray coach CWT7 saw regular service into the early 1980s but was then stored out of use before withdrawal in 1987. Repainted in the pale green livery with highly-stylised Chipman logo adopted during the mid-1970s, it appears in picture three.

Five more weedkilling vehicles, two staff and dormitory coaches and three spray coaches, followed between 1963 and 1965, allowing the last of the 1950s conversions to be retired. Lack of space precludes the illustration of each of these vehicles but spray coach CWT9 and staff and dormitory coach CWT10 have been selected as representative.

Like CWT7, spray coach CWT9 was converted from a Southern BTK of Maunsell design (picture four). Although the similarity is obvious, there are clear differences too, the most obvious being the number of windows and doors and the length of the guard's area, both resulting from the fact that, whereas CWT7 was a converted four-compartment brake third, CWT9 was a modification of the six-compartment variant. Renumbered CC99009, it remained in regular use until 1988. Staff and dormitory coach CWT10 (picture five), which later became CC99010, survived in regular use until 1980 but was not condemned until 1984.

Converted at the same time and from coaches of the same design, CWT11 and CWT12 were identical to CWT9 and CWT10 respectively, being renumbered as CC99011 and CC99012. In 1977, CC99012 was withdrawn and CC99011 was relegated to become a spare spray coach but saw little further use and was condemned in 1981. Converted as the original spare spray coach, CWT13 (CC99013) saw little, if any, use, and was withdrawn in 1978.

The final development in the fleet of coaches used by Chipman's in its vacuum-braked weedkilling trains took place in 1981, when the company introduced a spray van, CC99014, and staff and dormitory coach, CC9015, converted from former Southern Railway scenery vans. These vehicles (picture six) entered service in plain green but subsequently received a revised Chipman logo, an embellishment that was applied to the coaches but not the tank wagons during the mid-1980s.

ABOVE: Picture four: Showing its much smaller brake area, spray coach CC 99009 (ex CWT9) was found at Watford Junction on May 17, 1980 and displaying the highly-stylised Chipman logo. Donald Farmborough/Trevor Mann Collection

ABOVE: Picture five: Staff and dormitory coach CC99010 (previously CWT10) was also at Watford Junction on May 17, 1980. In this livery style, the lettering was arranged to display 'Chipman weed control' on each side of the train, thus on the other side, CC99010 carried 'Chipman' while CC99009 featured the 'weed control' lettering. Donald Farmborough/Trevor Mann Collection

ABOVE: Picture three: In the revised green livery, spray coach CC99007 (previously CWT7) was stabled at Horsham on July 31, 1979. Donald Farmborough/Trevor Mann Collection

ABOVE: Picture six: Taken at Horsham on April 5, 1987, spray van CC99014 displays the revised Chipman logo. The modifications included creating a revised section of bodywork to mount the spraying equipment on and an adjacent operator's position to give a better view of the track and spray application. Andy Prime

Modelling BR Departmental Coaching Stock **95**

Weeding the network

ABOVE: **Picture seven:** Large quantities of water were required for the spraying operation to mix with the herbicide. In the plain version of the Chipman green livery, CC48119 (originally BRT47258) was to be found at Watford Junction on May 17, 1980. *Donald Farmborough/Trevor Mann Collection*

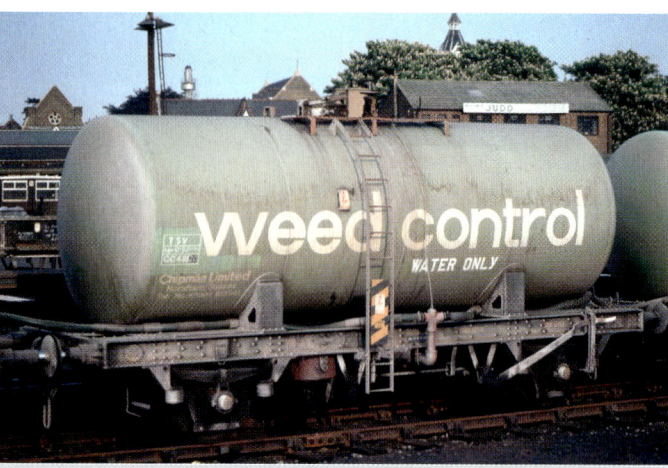

ABOVE: **Picture eight:** On the same day, CC48120 was still displaying the branding remnants of the initial green livery along with a number of design differences to its fellow tanker, both coded TSV. They were accompanied by coaches CC99009 and CC99010. *Donald Farmborough/Trevor Mann Collection*

Tanker types

Turning to the tank wagons that worked with these coaches, the anchor mounted vehicles have already been noted. There were over 50 of these wagons built in several batches between 1952 and 1957. The survivors were withdrawn together in 1975 but had probably seen little use for some years previously. The fleet was augmented in 1957 with a batch of four 35-ton GLW vacuum-braked tank wagons, which were built by Hurst Nelson to a design similar to that of the pioneering Esso tanks of the same year. Numbered 111-114, these vehicles worked in 'Train 4', illustrated in pictures one and two, and survived until 1977, by then carrying TOPS numbers of CC48111-14.

The next development saw a further six tank wagons of broadly similar design, numbered CC48115-20, purchased secondhand in 1973. Picture seven illustrates CC48119, a typical example that had been built by Powell Duffryn in 1959 as part of a batch of 34 Class A tankers originally hired to Mobil. Curiously, although BR records show all six as being drawn from that batch, CC48120 was actually an odd one out. Shown in picture eight, this had previously been TEX47828, built by Charles Roberts in 1960 for the Regent Oil Company. These pictures reveal several differences, including the tank mountings, but the shorter barrel is the most noticeable.

Having entered service in the green livery featuring 'Chipman' and 'weed control' lettering carried by CC48120, these vehicles passed through the plain green, exemplified by CC48119, before being repainted during the mid-1980s in the plain black livery that was also used for later air-braked tankers.

The final batch of vacuum-braked tanks, CC48441-44, were bought secondhand from Esso in 1977, presumably to replace CC48111-14. These were also 35-ton GLW tankers of late 1950s vintage so, curiously, were almost identical to the vehicles they superseded! Illustrated in picture nine, CC48443 was typical and had been built by Powell Duffryn in 1958. These wagons were never fully repainted, the Esso number being clearly visible. What might, at first sight, be taken to be Chipman's pale green was in fact an accumulation of herbicide spray drift.

ABOVE: **Picture nine:** Formerly ESSO48341, July 31, 1979, found CC48443 in its revised water carrying role at Horsham. Invariably, the herbicide spray tended to coat the vehicles nearest to the nozzles in grot. *Donald Farmborough/Trevor Mann Collection*

Third phase

A major shake-up of weedkilling train provision followed the 1988 campaign. The Eastern Region 'in house' operation ceased with the territories covered by Chipman and Schering adjusted so that, between them, they reached the entire network. From the 1989 season, each contractor operated a single air-braked train powered by hired-in Hunslet-Barclay Class 20/9 locomotives. This led to the withdrawal of CC99008 and C99009, the last surviving Chipman coaches of the mid-1960s. The water tanks were also taken out of weedkilling use, although some saw further use in the company's drain cleaning train.

The first step in the creation of the new weedkilling train saw the two modified scenery vans, CC99014 and CC99015, fitted with air brakes at New Cross Gate. For the start of the 1989 season, they were joined by CC99016. The first Mk.1 coach to be included in the Chipman train, it had been modified at RFS Industries, Doncaster. This formation is illustrated in picture ten. For much of the 1989 and 1990 campaigns, a hired-in BR ferry van, Civil Engineers' grey/yellow DB786951, was also included in the train as a stores van, this also gaining the temporary number of CC99017.

The train was repainted prior to the 1992 season, its new two-tone grey livery being relieved by orange and green stripes and, reflecting a recent change of ownership, Nomix-Chipman brandings and logos. Spray van CC99014 and staff, store, and dormitory coach CC99016 are shown in the revised colours in pictures 11 and 12.

A further three new conversions entered service with Nomix-Chipman during the early-1990s so that by 1994, the company was operating a train formed of four modified Mk.1 coaches, as detailed in table two. Their arrival allowed the retirement of the former scenery vans

Weeding the network

ABOVE: **Picture ten:** During April 1990, 20901 *Nancy* and 20904 *Janis* arrive at Churston while spraying the Dartmouth Steam Railway as part of Chipman's campaign in the West Country. It was not unusual for weedkilling trains to work over heritage railways connected to the BR network. This photo also shows that the two newly air-braked scenery bans retained their original green paintwork into the 1990s and that CC99016 was turned out in the livery following conversion. *Trevor Mann Collection*

ABOVE: **Picture 11:** Showing the revised two-tone grey Chipman livery, spray coach CC99014 is seen to the north of Aylesbury station on August 12, 1992 on what was then the freight-only line to Calvert. *David Ratcliffe*

ABOVE: **Picture 12:** The first Mk.1 to be added to the train was a new staff, stores, and dormitory coach CC99016, this being a significant step up in accommodation. This is also seen at Aylesbury in August 1992, having initially appeared from conversion in the green livery. *David Ratcliffe*

ABOVE: **Picture 13:** Also at Aylesbury on August 12, 1992, staff, and dormitory coach CC99017 had joined the train for the 1990 season with CC99018 following in 1991. Both carried the green livery as a result before the grey repaint was carried out. *David Ratcliffe*

ABOVE: **Picture 14:** Once again photographed at Aylesbury in August 1992, TTA water tank CC55528 had previously been numbered VIP55218 and, following the sale of the fleet to Procor, PR55218. The parabolic springs date from the refurbishment of these wagons for Chipman's use, while the circular 'shadow' on the side of the barrel reveals the position of the VIP logo applied when these wagons were new. *David Ratcliffe*

CC99014 and CC99015, although both were subsequently used on autumn 'leaf-buster' workings. CC99017, the staff and dormitory coach that replaced CC99015 following modification at Cardiff Cathays in mid-1990, is illustrated in picture 13, while CC99018 and CC99019 followed in 1991 and 1994, respectively.

The formation of the new set was rounded off by three or four air-braked water tanks, drawn from a fleet of five 45-ton GLW Class A tank wagons purchased secondhand from CAIB in 1986 (picture 14). Numbered CC55526-30, these had been built by Standard Wagon in 1966/67 as part of a batch of 44 vehicles for VIP Petroleum. These tankers were then replaced prior to the 1996 season by four TTAs numbered STL55514-19 and hired from EG Steele. These were easily distinguishable because of their pedestal suspension and blue barrels and remained in use throughout 1996 and 1997.

The air-braked Nomix-Chipman train continued in service, working over Southern, Western and Scottish regions, until the close of the 1997 weed-control campaign, when it fell victim to a further restructuring that saw AgrEvo awarded a nationwide contract for the following year. As a result, the four Mk.1s were sold off almost immediately, CC99016-18 to Balfour Beatty as already detailed and CC99019 to Railtrack. Scenery vans CC99014 and CC9015 languished at Horsham until 2011 and now reside at the Isle of Wight Steam Railway. Sadly, both are intended as underframe donors to go under vintage coach bodies with CC99015 reduced to its chassis in 2014 but CC99014 retains most of its modified body and Chipman livery for now.

Table two: Chipman air-braked coaches, TOPS code KCA

Number	Design Code	Vehicle Type
CC99016	PP028A/KC028A	Staff, store & dormitory coach
Ex Mk. 1 BCK 21275, built Derby 1964 to BR diagram 172. Briefly coded PPA initially.		
CC99017	KC032A	Staff & dormitory coach
Ex Mk. 1 TSO 4066 built Ashford/Swindon 1956-57 to BR diagram 93.		
CC99018	KC033B	Generator & chemical stores coach
Ex Mk. 1 TSO 4393 built Ashford/Swindon 1957 to BR diagram 93.		
CC99019	KC033C	Spray coach
Ex BR Mk. 1 RMB 1870, built Wolverton 1962 to BR diagram 99.		

Modelling BR Departmental Coaching Stock 97

Weeding the network

Creating the Chipman by Tom Curtis

ABOVE: Spray coach CC99014 was the most difficult vehicle of the project, it being a largely scratchbuilt model with various kit components added. This angle shows the operator's spraying position to advantage while the large diameter hose running to the water tanks can be seen on the solebar. All photographs by Gareth Bayer

In 2009, Kernow Model Rail Centre released a pair of OO gauge limited edition Bachmann Class 20s in Hunslet Barclay colours, this was followed by a set of the black-liveried water tank TTAs. The release of the locos and tankers lead to research into and subsequent modelling of the coaches as running in 1992, the first year in two-tone grey. In this weedkilling season, the spray coach was still former scenery van CC99014 and the three supporting Mk.1 coaches CC99016-18. Ready-to-run representations of two of the coaches were subsequently released but these lacked any of the necessary modifications to accurately depict the vehicles.

Staff & dormitory CC99017
The first vehicle to be tackled was the mess coach, which started life as a Mk.1 TSO.

To produce the model, a Bachmann TSO was dismantled with the underframe being completely stripped of all its components. A variety of gas bottle storage cabinets and other boxes were scratchbuilt and put in place, while also added to the underframe was air brake equipment and external handbrake wheels, the latter being a Stenson Models product. The handbrake was a feature of all the Chipman coaches, so all required this alteration.

The bodysides remained largely unchanged apart from the toilet windows, these being replaced with a single piece of glass on one side and removed completely on the other. Two square vents for the heating system were also added between two windows on one side. The most notable change was the complete removal of one of the gangway connections with replacement communication equipment made up from fine wire and new lamp irons added from the Shawplan range.

The interior is an impression based upon descriptions and exterior photos of the real thing. The venetian blinds were made from heavily scored styrene sheet which was glued behind the glazing.

Staff, stores and dormitory CC99016
Formerly a Mk.1 BCK, this vehicle had each of its compartments converted into sleeping accommodation. The former toilet between the brake area and the compartments became a shower facility with the other toilet housing a washing machine and tumble dryer. The brake compartment gave way to a locker room and workbench.

Weeding the network

With the donor models all being earlier Bachmann Mk.1s, the over-scale roof ribs were all sanded down and the roof vents replaced with the correct scallop dome type from MJT, some also requiring repositioning to suit the specific coaches.

The most noticeable change on the bodysides was the removal of the passenger doors nearest the brake end. This was modelled using blank coach sides from another scrap Bachmann Mk.1 spliced into the BCK sides with the joints being filled and sanded. On one side, the door was replaced with two square vents which were recessed into the body while there were also recessed vents underneath four of the compartment windows.

The underframe was modified with the removal of any vacuum brake equipment (the whole weedkilling train was air brake only) and then battery boxes, two scratchbuilt gas bottle cabinets and handbrakes were added. On the coach ends, electrical junction boxes were fitted, these featuring on all the Chipman coaches to provide additional electrical connections between them.

Generator & stores CC99018

The chemical stores coach also began life as a Bachmann TSO and saw the most noticeable changes to the body exterior with the addition of a roller shutter door on each side. These were cut from the etched sides of a Hurst Models Super GUV conversion and spliced into the Bachmann sides in the appropriate positions.

New window frames were added to all

BELOW: **The easiest of the Mk.1 conversions was CC99017, this having relatively few bodyside alterations. Most notable are the plethora of gas cylinder cabinets on the underframe and the rebuilt interior.**

Modelling BR Departmental Coaching Stock 99

Weeding the network

ABOVE: CC99016 shows the blank mid-body section where a passenger door used to be while the dormitory compartments can also be seen through the windows. The underframe was sparse on this vehicle, but the external handbrake wheel stands out.

three vehicles to represent the raised frames fitted to many Mk.1 coaches during their lives, these coming from Southern Pride Models. Supplied in the form of self-adhesive vinyls, they were carefully added to the window apertures before painting. All of the glazing on this coach was removed with the door droplight windows being filled in with plastic sheet while the rest of the glazing was overpainted with the grey body colour where required before refitting.

The underframe was once again cleared of everything, and two large rectangular fuel tanks added at one end along with the external handbrake and another small box at the other end. On the ends of the coach, the toilet water tank filler pipes were removed, as they also were on CC99017.

All of the Mk.1s were finished off with correct length stepboards fitted along the solebars as were painted representations of the yellow TOPS registration plates, while steps were added to the bogies where applicable. All of the plastic buffers were replaced with cast whitemetal retracted coach buffers from Comet Models. The exception to this was the non-gangway end of CC99017, which received cast extended buffers, again from Comet, as this end was always coupled to a loco.

Spray coach CC99014

The spray coach was without a doubt the hardest vehicle to research and produce. With no ready-to-run model or kit available for the Southern scenery van, there was no choice but to find and measure the real thing. At the time, the coach still survived at Nomix-Chipman's former base in Horsham Yard. Now part of a Network Rail infrastructure depot, permission was sought and granted to enter the site to measure and photograph the now derelict coach. Once the measurements were taken, a drawing was produced, and this acted as a guide for construction.

The coach sides started as two rectangles of thick styrene sheet to act as a base. The doors were cut from a Parkside Southern Railway BY utility van kit and added to the sides along with various bits of Microstrip to represent the body framing. Window apertures were cut out and then the floor put in place, with lots of thick box section added to keep the body square and prevent warping.

The underframe, bogies and buffers came from Ratio's Southern Van B utility van kit with additional weight added using little

ABOVE: Displaying a more involved external conversion, CC99018 was used to store the various chemicals and positioned next to the spraying vehicle. Besides the roller shutter door, it also had its windows painted over and a large fuel tank fitted to the underframe, this feeding the generator set carried by the coach.

Weeding the network

fishing weights, although liquid lead would have done the same job. The real van had a gangway added, made with large folds of rubber, at one end only to give access to the chemical stores coach. On the model, this was replicated by using lengths of thin plastic vinyl cut from a door blind, which was folded round and glued. Once the bogies had been added, additional detail followed, such as the stepboards, air tanks (taken from a Lima Seacow ballast hopper) and etched handbrake wheels.

The large, curved roof was formed from two lengths of wooden quadrant with plastic box section in-between. This was then layered with plastic sheet and filed to shape. The roof ribs were made from the thinnest Microstrip available, which was held in place and then quickly brushed with Plastic Weld. The rainstrips over the doors were sourced from the aforementioned Ratio kit.

Following painting, the windows could be added using the glazing from old Lima Mk.1s, purely as it was easy to work with. It was trimmed to size and then friction fitted into the apertures, being held in place with Johnsons Klear floor polish.

The large diameter pipe which fed from the TTA water tanks and ran the length of the spray coach was formed from electrical wire with copper strands removed. This was done to make it much more flexible, but it could also be made from thin brass wire to give it shape where necessary. Two Shawplan Class 60 air horns were added at the non-gangway end of the coach while the lamp irons on the end and along the sides of the coach were made from flattened brass handrail wire.

TTA tankers

The Kernow limited edition pack of TTAs contained four wagons, although only three were required for this version of the train. While the livery and numbers were accurate, some of the underframe details along with the walkways were not correct for the type of TTA used in the Nomix-Chipman train. To improve the look, the leaf springs on the model were cut away and replaced with cast whitemetal parabolic springs from S-Kits.

The walkways were modified by removing the moulded items and then cutting and rearranging them into a pattern that was much closer to the actual tanks. As a consequence, the end ladders also needed replacing with etched versions, while the filler pipe at the opposite end of the barrel was simply added using brass wire. The large diameter water pipe that ran along each side of the tanks and fed the spray coach was again formed from electrical wire.

Livery

The two shades of grey used along with the transfers were supplied by Scale Model Transfers, which is unfortunately no longer trading. Looking through photos of the Chipman set, these showed it in a whole range of weathered conditions. The result of the chemical spraying tended to give the train, including the locos, a very white weathered appearance and often this was so bad that the livery could not be seen underneath. Additionally, if the train had spent much of its time travelling in the same direction, then one end would be whiter than the other.

However, as it was cleaned fairly regularly, I settled for just a light dusting so that the underlying livery could be seen. Photos also revealed that the tops of the TTAs, which did not get reached by the cleaning, had a green tinge to them. Other painted details included the white 'slip' marks found on the wheels, which were added using a Bob Moore lining pen.

Although there are many photographs of this train in service, the only way to get certain details correct was to go and measure and photograph the real thing. The project would not have been possible without the help of Network Rail and the Gloucestershire-Warwickshire Railway. I would also like to thank Paul Wade, Adrian Full, Mark Begley, Martyn Normanton, Alan Barrow and Andi Dell for their help with this model.

RIGHT: The Kernow TTA models all received modified walkways to better portray the variant carried by the real tankers as well as new ladders, correct pattern parabolic springs and suitable weathering. The flexible water hoses on the solebars and filler pipe to the top hatch complete the modifications.

The full Nomix-Chipman weedkilling set is seen in action on the author's now sold-on Northolt International layout as it threads its way through the suburbs of northwest London. In the background is an offshoot of the London Underground's Central Line.

Modelling BR Departmental Coaching Stock

Weeding the network

Fisons Weedkillers

ABOVE: Picture one. The Mk VI version of the Fisons weedkiller was notable for utilising a Class 100 Driving Trail Composite as its spray coach. Photographed stabled at Reading in July 1979, the amount of equipment installed on the underframe of what was now FA99900 is evident while the spray nozzles are positioned by the leading bogie. Behind it are former GWR BG stores vans FA99901 and FA99902 with staff coach FA99904 at the rear.
Simon Bendall Collection

The origins of the Fisons Agrochemical Division can be traced back to 1939 when Pest Control Ltd began manufacturing herbicides and pesticides at Hauxton, to the south of Cambridge. This company was acquired by Fisons Ltd in 1954 as part of its post-war diversification away from fertiliser manufacture, becoming Fisons Pest Control Ltd and then from 1970, Fisons Ltd Agrochemical Division.

The firm first entered the railway weed-control business in 1957. Little is known of its early operations but by 1963, the company was operating two trains, referred to as the Mark III and Mark IIIa. Photographs reveal that the latter, which worked over the London Midland Region, comprised a modified ex-LMS coach accompanied by ex-LMS steam locomotive tenders. The Mark III train was probably similar. Development continued and by 1969 these trains had been replaced by the Mk IVa and Mk V sets, each consisting of two modified ex-LMS coaches (including those used previously), one being the spray coach, and the other a staff and dormitory vehicle. Hired 45-ton GLW tank wagons had superseded the tenders used previously.

A Mark VI train, which replaced the existing Mk V train and would remain in service until 1989, was introduced in 1975, soon after Fisons had adopted an attractive green and yellow livery. Seen in picture one, this consisted of a staff and dormitory coach, two stores vans and a spray coach, as detailed in the table.

Staff and dormitory coach FA99904 (picture two) was the only vehicle to be retained from the Mk V train, it also keeping the enamelled boards that proclaimed 'Fisons Limited Agrochemical Division' and 'Weed Control Services' that had featured on an earlier white livery. The tank wagon, lettered for use by Dow Chemicals, is also noteworthy.

Two newly acquired stores vans were also included in the train, FA99902 (picture three) being recorded at Foxton in April

Table one: Fisons vacuum-braked coaches, TOPS code PPV			
Tops No.	BR Diagram	Design Code	Vehicle Type
FA99900	6/900	PP020A	Spray coach, Mk VI train
Ex BR Class 100 DTCL 56315, built Gloucester RC&W 1957 to BR diagram 537.			
FA99901	6/901	PP021A	Stores van, Mk VI train
Ex GWR Gangwayed BG W150W, built Swindon 1936 to GWR diagram K41.			
FA99902	6/905	PP022A	Stores van, Mk VI train
Ex GWR Gangwayed BG W164W, built Swindon 1937 to GWR diagram K42.			
FA99903	6/902	PP023A	Spray coach, Mk IV train
Ex LMS Stanier vestibule TO, identity not known, built Wolverton 1945 to LMS diagram 1999.			
FA99904	6/903	PP024A	Staff & dormitory coach, Mk VI train
Ex LMS Ivatt TK M2156M, built Derby 1946 to LMS diagram 2119.			
FA99905	6/904	PP025A	Staff & dormitory coach, Mk IV train
Ex LMS Ivatt 'Porthole' BTK, identity not known, built Wolverton 1950 to LMS diagram 2161.			
FA99906	n/a	PP026A	Stores van, Mk IV train
Ex GWR Gangwayed BG W70W, built Swindon 1941 to GWR diagram K44.			

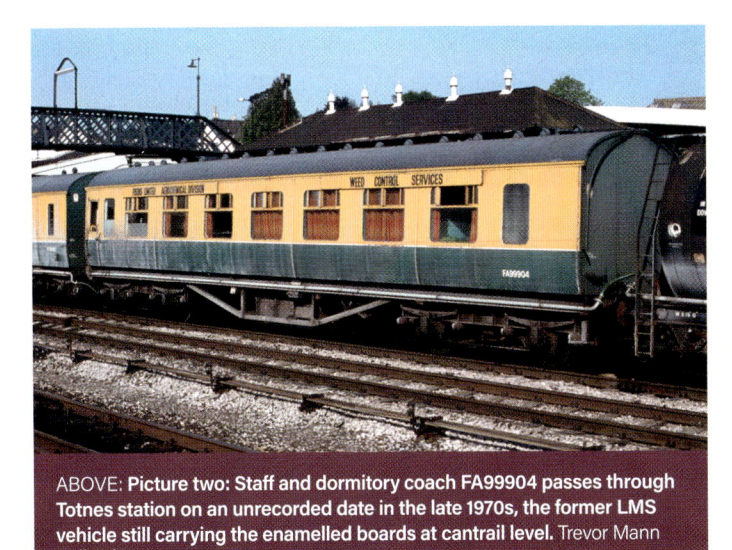

Weeding the network

ABOVE: **Picture two:** Staff and dormitory coach FA99904 passes through Totnes station on an unrecorded date in the late 1970s, the former LMS vehicle still carrying the enamelled boards at cantrail level. *Trevor Mann Collection*

ABOVE: **Picture three:** Ex Great Western stores van FA99902 was residing at Foxton on April 12, 1979, this being a convenient base of operations for the Cambridgeshire-based company. *Trevor Mann*

1979, which was the operating base for the Fisons trains at this time. By way of contrast, FA99901 (picture four) was found at Castleton permanent way depot, which was a regular stabling point when the train was working in Manchester and southeast Lancashire. By the June 1983 date of this photo, Fisons had merged its agrochemical business with that of Boots to create a new company, FBC Ltd, and this had resulted in the train being repainted into a new but equally attractive red and white livery. The most unusual feature of the Mk VI train though was undoubtedly its spray coach, a modified Class 100 DMU trailer, which is seen in picture five.

The earlier Mark IVa train commissioned in 1966 was repainted into the yellow and green livery in the early 1970s and continued in service alongside the new Mk VI set. Illustrated in picture six, at this 1973 date it included three ex-LNER/BR fish vans which provided storage space for bagged herbicides. Its dedicated stores van FA99906 was not introduced until 1979 and this would remain in BR blue until the train was repainted into red and white during the early 1980s (picture seven). During this period, the Mark IVa train spent much of its time working across the Scottish Region

ABOVE: **Picture four:** In the revised red and white colours, the second former GWR Full Brake stores van FA99901 was stabled at Castleton on June 6, 1983. *Trevor Mann*

ABOVE: **Picture five:** Also photographed in June 1983 at Castleton was spray coach FA99900, its red and white livery carrying the FBC Limited logo of its new operator and what appears to be a royal warrant on the adjacent door. Note the sliding window fitted above the spray jets and number to provide the operator with a good view. *Trevor Mann*

ABOVE: **Picture six:** The older Mk IVa Fisons weedkiller passes through Faversham in July 1973 with 33062 in charge. Now in the green and yellow livery, the former fish vans used for storage are just coming into view behind the dormitory coach. *David Monk-Steel*

ABOVE: **Picture seven:** A Class 33 was again in charge of the older Mk IVa weedkiller as it traverses the Fawley branch at Totton on May 10, 1984, behind 33032. This was now in red and white under the ownership of FBC Limited and made up to three coaches with the addition of ex GWR stores vehicle FA99906 between spray coach FA99903 and dormitory FA99905. *Trevor Mann Collection*

Modelling BR Departmental Coaching Stock **103**

Weeding the network

ABOVE: Picture eight: Illustrating the type of TTA hired from BP for use as a water tank, BPO66294 is seen at Castleton on June 16, 1983, while being re-filled. *Trevor Mann*

ABOVE: Picture nine: FA56960, which was stabled at Castleton on May 15, 1986, had previously been BPO60162, built by RY Pickering in 1965. *David Ratcliffe*

but also sprayed parts of the Southern and Eastern, leaving the Mark VI set allocated primarily to the London Midland.

Tanker details

Although they had previously featured several different types of tanker, including Algeco ferry tanks, the Fisons trains of the late 1970s and early 1980s invariably used hired BP 45-ton Class B tank wagons as the water tanks. At least 17 examples were used over the years but BPO66294 (picture eight), built by RY Pickering in 1965, was typical.

In 1985, a change of policy saw FBC Ltd purchase six tank wagons from BP. Renumbered FA56960-65, these were 45-ton GLW vacuum-braked Class A vehicles with Epikote lining for aviation fuel traffic. As well as an internal clean, these received a coat of grey paint with red branding (picture nine).

Following the 1986 acquisition of FBC Ltd by Schering Agrochemicals, both Mk IVa and Mk VI trains were repainted into the emerald colours of their new owner. They operated in this condition during the 1987 and 1988 campaigns, although FA99902 was withdrawn following fire damage in early 1988, reducing the Mk VI train to a three-coach set. They were withdrawn following the 1988 weedkilling season, with just tankers FA56960-62 being retained for use in a new train.

The Schering train

Schering Agrochemicals introduced a new air-braked weedkilling train for the start of the 1989 campaign (picture ten). Top

ABOVE: Picture ten: Like the Chipman set, Hunslet-Barclay Class 20/9 power came to what was now the Schering weedkilling train from the 1989 season. The usual duo were 20902 *Lorna* and 20903 *Alison* with the former seen stabled at Watford Junction on April 28, 1990. The initial green livery as applied to the TTA water tanks is also apparent. *Trevor Mann Collection*

and tailed by Class 20/9 locos hired from Hunslet-Barclay, this was a product of RFS Industries at Doncaster and featured four modified Mk.1 coaches and three refurbished water tanks.

The most heavily modified vehicle in the new set was SA99908 (picture 11), the generator and stores coach, which was rebuilt in the style of a breakdown train tool van with virtually no windows left and alerted doors. Rather more recognisable as a former passenger Mk.1 was SA99910 (picture 12), the dormitory coach for the train. Upon conversion, the set carried the original Schering livery of emerald bodywork with a white waistline stripe.

As shown in picture 13, spray coach FA99907 was marshalled adjacent to the water tanks, the spray nozzles being visible at the far end of the coach, below the sliding windows that allowed the operator a clear view of both track and spray jets. FA99909, the staff and workshop coach (picture 14), provided kitchen and lounge facilities for the on-board staff, together with a small workshop used to make running repairs to the equipment. By the time these photographs were taken in July 1995, Schering and Hoechst had merged their crop protection businesses into a joint venture, Hoechst Schering AgrEvo GmbH, and the train had been repainted into the turquoise-green colours of its new owners.

The three tank wagons that had been allocated to the Mk VI train, SA56960-62, were retained for use in the new air-braked set. Already repainted into emerald prior to the 1987 campaign, these were now fitted with air brakes and parabolic springs; SA56961 and SA56962 appear in this condition in picture ten while SA56961

Table two: Schering air-braked coaches, TOPS code PPA then KCA		
Tops No.	Design Code	Vehicle Type
SA99907	PP029A/KC029A	Spray coach
Ex Mk.1 CK 7203 (originally 16203), built Derby 1961 to BR diagram 128.		
SA99908	PP030A/KC030A	Generator & stores coach
Ex Mk.1 CK 7160 (originally 16160), built Derby 1961 to BR diagram 126.		
SA99909	PP031A/KC031A	Staff & workshop coach
Ex Mk 1 SK 18401 (originally 25401), built Wolverton 1957 to BR diagram 146.		
SA99910	PP031B/KC031B	Dormitory coach
Ex Mk.1 SK 18574 (originally 25574), built Wolverton 1957 to BR diagram 146.		

Weeding the network

is illustrated in its later turquoise livery in picture 15.

Between 1989 and the close of the 1997 weed-control season, the Schering train worked across East Anglia and the former Eastern and London Midland regions, with Chipman's being responsible for Scottish, Southern and Western routes. Following a competitive tendering process, AgrEvo was then awarded a nationwide contract for the 1998 and 1999 seasons, and at the same time terminated its traction agreement with Hunslet-Barclay in favour of EWS as can be seen in picture 16.

The arrival of a sizeable fleet of Railtrack Multi-Purpose Vehicles resulted in 2000 being the last year of operation for the AgrEvo set. Following the end of that year's weed-control campaign, the coaches and tankers were initially put into storage at Doncaster Works and then an industrial site at Selby, and later exported to Belgium where, operated by Weedfree Ltd, they survived until 2007.

ABOVE: Picture 11: You would be hard-pressed to tell SA99908 was originally a Mk.1 Composite Corridor (CK) following its rebuilding as a generator and stores coach, this being recorded at Castleton in the initial green livery on September 16, 1990. Trevor Mann

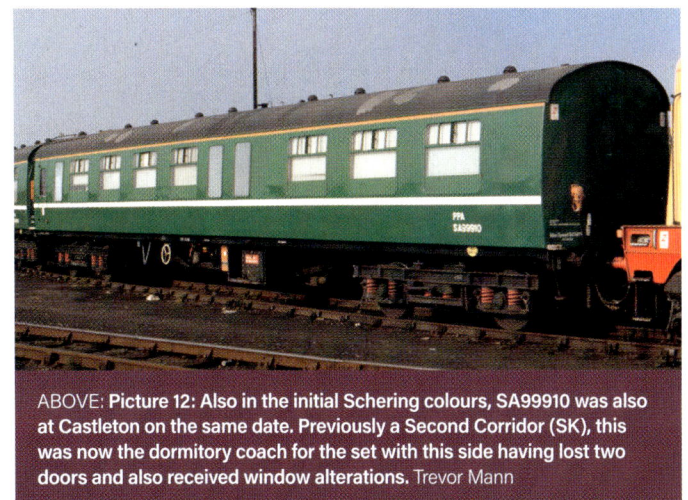

ABOVE: Picture 12: Also in the initial Schering colours, SA99910 was also at Castleton on the same date. Previously a Second Corridor (SK), this was now the dormitory coach for the set with this side having lost two doors and also received window alterations. Trevor Mann

ABOVE: Picture 13: Spray coach SA99907 was equipped with a roller shutter door on each side, albeit not in the same place, to allow easy access for equipment and materials. The nearer windows also provide a glimpse of the mixing tanks and pumping equipment inside. The revised turquoise livery is on show at Castleton in July 1995. Trevor Mann

ABOVE: Picture 14: The last Mk.1 included in this weedkiller train was staff and workshop coach SA99909, a former Second Corridor which was also at Castleton in May 1995. The nearest end housed the staff facilities with blinds provided for privacy and even a TV aerial clipped to the rainstrip in those pre-digital days! Trevor Mann

ABOVE: Picture 15: The later turquoise colour looked particularly fetching on TTA SA56961 at Castleton on the same date. Like all weedkilling trains, external pipe runs of both fixed and flexible types were fitted between the tankers and spray coach to ensure a continuous supply of water while on the move. Trevor Mann

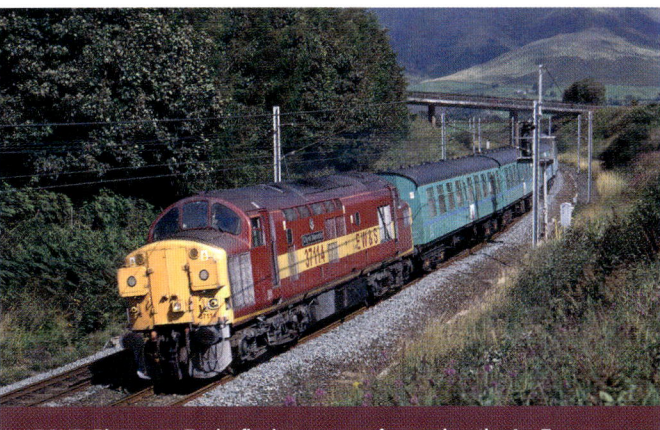

ABOVE: Picture 16: For its final two years of operation, the AgrEvo weedkiller as it was known by this time was hauled by EWS traction, this invariably being a pair of Class 37s in top and tail formation. Although the locos came from a colourful selection, 37114 *City of Worcester* was a frequent choice and is seen leading the formation at Beckfoot on August 15, 1998. Out of sight at the rear was Mainline Freight blue 37023 *Stratford TMD Quality Approved*. David Dockray

Modelling BR Departmental Coaching Stock **105**

Weeding the network

Railtrack Weedkillers

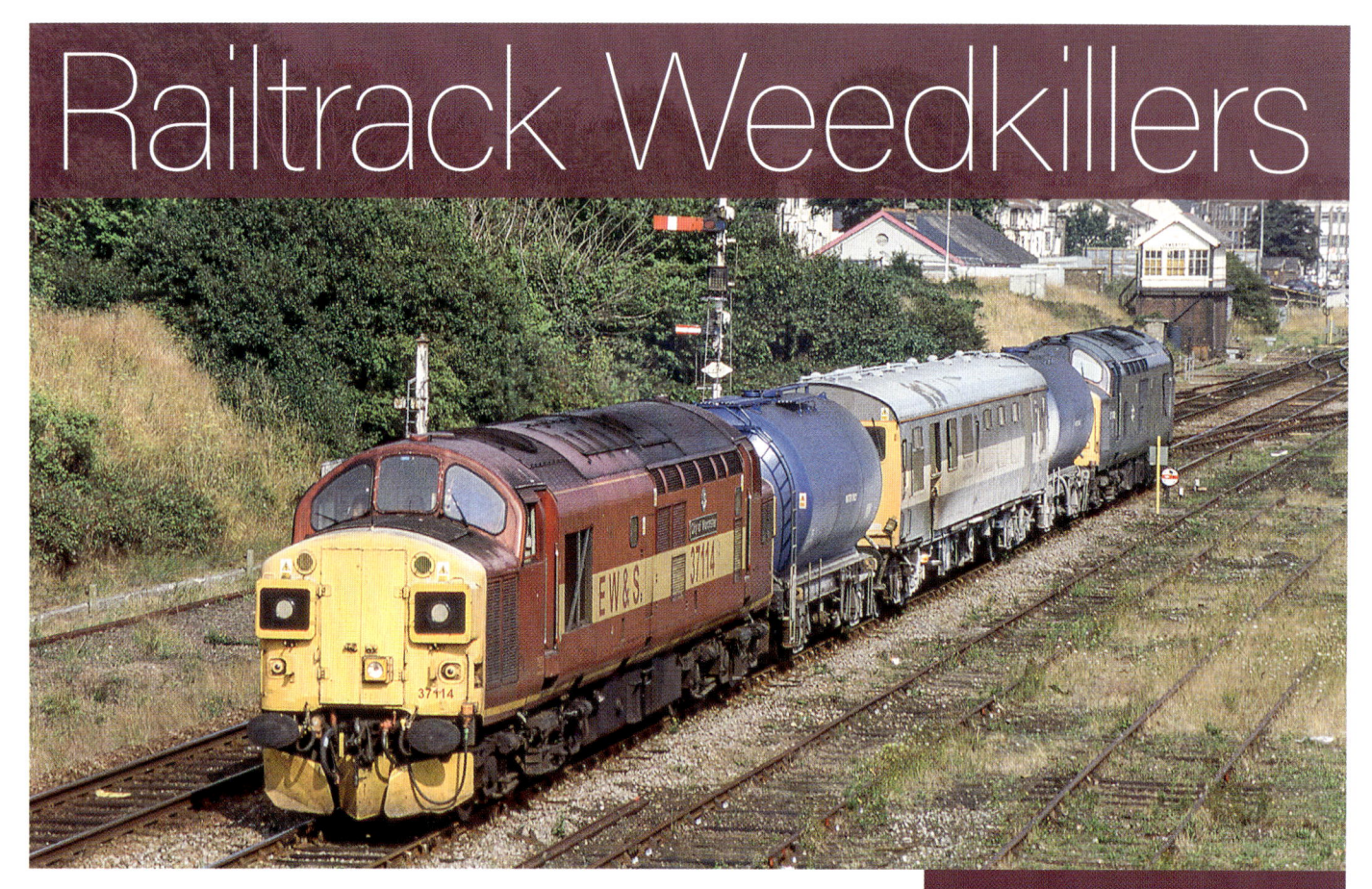

The 1999 weed-control season saw an increase in rolling stock resources following a poor campaign the previous year when the AgrEvo loco-hauled set was expected to cover the whole of the UK on its own. Unsurprisingly, this left many lines under-treated with resultant media criticism of Railtrack on the state of the network. Two new trains were therefore prepared in time for the 1999 season starting that April.

The first of these was Mk.1-based spray coach 99019 (the CC prefix now dropped), which was acquired by Railtrack following the withdrawal of the Chipman train. This was taken to Derby for overhaul and returned to traffic painted in a grey and white livery with Railtrack branding. Under the initial plans, it was intended to work as a centre vehicle between Geismar VMT860 vehicles DR98305 and DR98306 with these forerunners of the Multi-Purpose Vehicles modified to carry the water.

This method of operation proved to be short-lived, and the spray coach soon returned to top and tail loco haulage with EWS motive power. Water was sourced from an EG Steele blue-painted TTA tanker with a ZCA Sea Urchin also included in the formation, possibly for brake force purposes as it was never obviously loaded in photographs.

From 2003, a second TTA replaced the ZCA, while the following year saw more significant changes. Firstly, both TTAs were ousted by a KFA container flat, this carrying three of the blue-painted water tank modules that were then coming into use as part of the autumnal Railhead Treatment Trains. Secondly, 99019 received an all-over blue repaint but devoid of any branding.

In 2005, it was the traction that changed as EWS Class 37s gave way to Direct Rail Services locos, invariably a pair of Class 20/3s. This was the last year of the spray coach's use though and operations were increasingly nocturnal due to problems finding a path for a 30mph train spraying weedkiller during the day. Subsequently, 99019 was stored at York, Carnforth and then Long Marston but in early 2022, it was in poor condition and earmarked for scrapping.

Other solutions

The second new train introduced in 1999 was *Flower*, an adapted Class 141 Pacer with the former 141118 being finished in Serco red/grey. This was very much a stop-gap as again it could only spray herbicide at a maximum speed of 30mph and equally could only average around 30 miles of spraying before needing its water supply replenished; its lightweight construction preventing a heavier load being carried. Its use was short-lived with sale to Cotswold Rail coming in 2000 and export to Iran three years later.

From 2000 onwards, most of the network's weedkilling requirements were fulfilled by the new Windhoff Multi-Purpose (MPV) fleet, several of these spending the summer months fitted with weedkiller modules and traversing the network. This remains the case 22 years later but 2021/22 has seen Network Rail take delivery of a trio of new wagon-based weedkillers, each featuring three KFA flat wagons equipped with modules on top and to be hauled by GB Railfreight Class 66s. Utilising weed recognition software and computer-controlled spraying systems, these are being touted as a significant step forward in tackling the network's out of control vegetation as they enter full service this spring.

ABOVE: Former Chipman spray coach and now prefix-less 99019 is seen in action at Lowestoft on August 5, 2003, with EWS-liveried 37114 *City of Worcester* leading it away from the terminus and 'celebrity' BR blue example 37308 on the rear. This was the final season in which the coach would carry the obsolete Railtrack grey and white and see it operate with two EG Steele TTA water tanks. Gareth Bayer

ABOVE: Looking somewhat odd in Serco colours, 141118 *Flower* was a short-term solution to a lack of weedkilling vehicles in 1999, its spraying equipment being mounted around the couplings. Quite what the Iranian reaction to its arrival in the Middle East in 2003 was is anyone's guess! Colour-Rail

ABOVE: Once a Mk.1 Miniature Buffet (RMB), there was little left to betray 99019's origins at Norwich on August 26, 2005. This was its final year of operation, its second in the unbranded blue livery and its first with DRS traction, in this case English Electric Type 1s 20312 and 20313. Gareth Bayer

MAIL ORDER
Key Books

HORNBY MAGAZINE YEARBOOK NO.14 HARDBACK

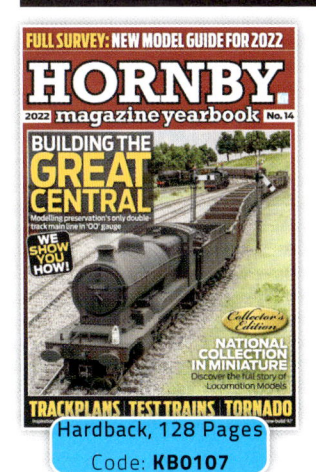

2022 Hardback Collector's Edition — *NEW*
The fourteenth edition of the *Hornby Magazine* Yearbook features 128 pages of model railway inspiration from the team behind Britain's magazine for modellers, written by modellers.

Hardback, 128 Pages
Code: **KB0107**

ONLY £17.99
Subscribers call for your £2 discount

IRISH RAILWAYS: THE LAST SIXTY YEARS

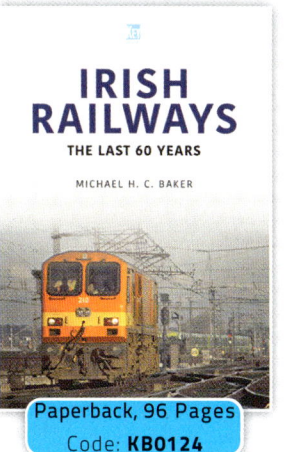

World Railways Series, Vol 4
This is a visual journey around the Emerald Isle, starting in the 1960s and moving through to modern times, showing the various traction, locomotives and stations that have made Ireland's railways what they are today.

Paperback, 96 Pages
Code: **KB0124**

ONLY £15.99
Subscribers call for your £2 discount

RAIL FREIGHT: SCOTLAND

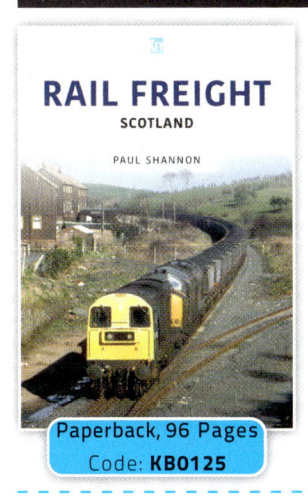

The Railways and Industry Series, Vol 6
With over 160 photographs, this volume looks at the changing face of rail freight in Scotland. It details the changes in traction, rolling stock and railway infrastructure over four decades.

Paperback, 96 Pages
Code: **KB0125**

ONLY £15.99
Subscribers call for your £2 discount

RAILWAYS OF SOUTH WEST SCOTLAND

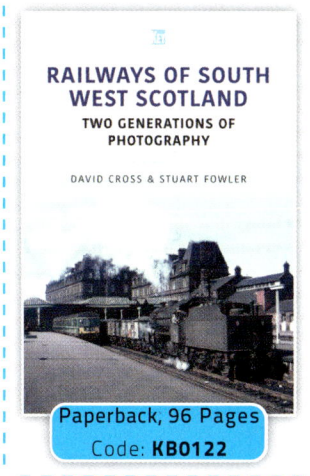

Britain's Railways Series, Vol 26
Exploring the region through the decades, this book is an invaluable reference for enthusiasts interested in the railways of the southwest of Scotland.

Paperback, 96 Pages
Code: **KB0122**

ONLY £15.99
Subscribers call for your £2 discount

CLASS 37S

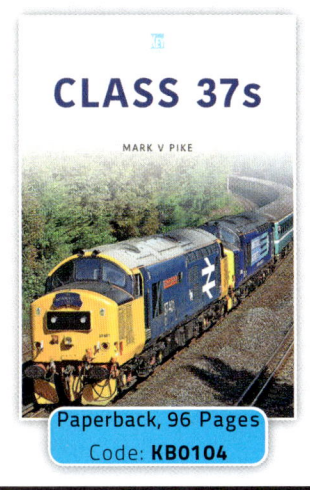

Britain's Railways Series, Volume 23
With over 200 images, this book is an illustrated celebration of Class 37s throughout the years.

Paperback, 96 Pages
Code: **KB0104**

ONLY £15.99
Subscribers call for your £2 discount

CLASS 442: THE WESSEX ELECTRICS

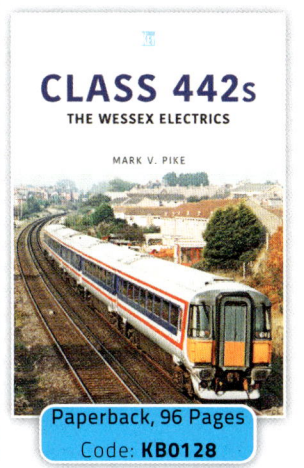

Britain's Railways Series, Vol 27
This book is a pictorial tribute of more than 200 images to what was, by far and away, the best electric unit ever to have worked on the Southern Region electrified lines.

Paperback, 96 Pages
Code: **KB0128**

ONLY £15.99
Subscribers call for your £2 discount

---

shop.keypublishing.com/books
Or call UK: **01780 480404** - Overseas: **+44 1780 480404**

Monday to Friday 9am-5:30pm GMT. Free 2nd class P&P on all UK & BFPO orders. Overseas charges apply.
All publication dates subject to change

TO VIEW OUR FULL RANGE OF BOOKS, VISIT OUR SHOP

019/22

The Official Book of Hornby's First 100 Years

HORNBY®
THE HORNBY BRAND IS A TRUE BRITISH ICON

As Hornby celebrates its Centenary year in 2020, here in one high-quality volume is a year-by-year account of the fortunes, successes and occasional failures of the famous model railway brand.

The story is told by model railway historian, collector and author, Pat Hammond, and includes over 800 illustrations of many of the models that have been produced over the years, including several which never made it into full production.

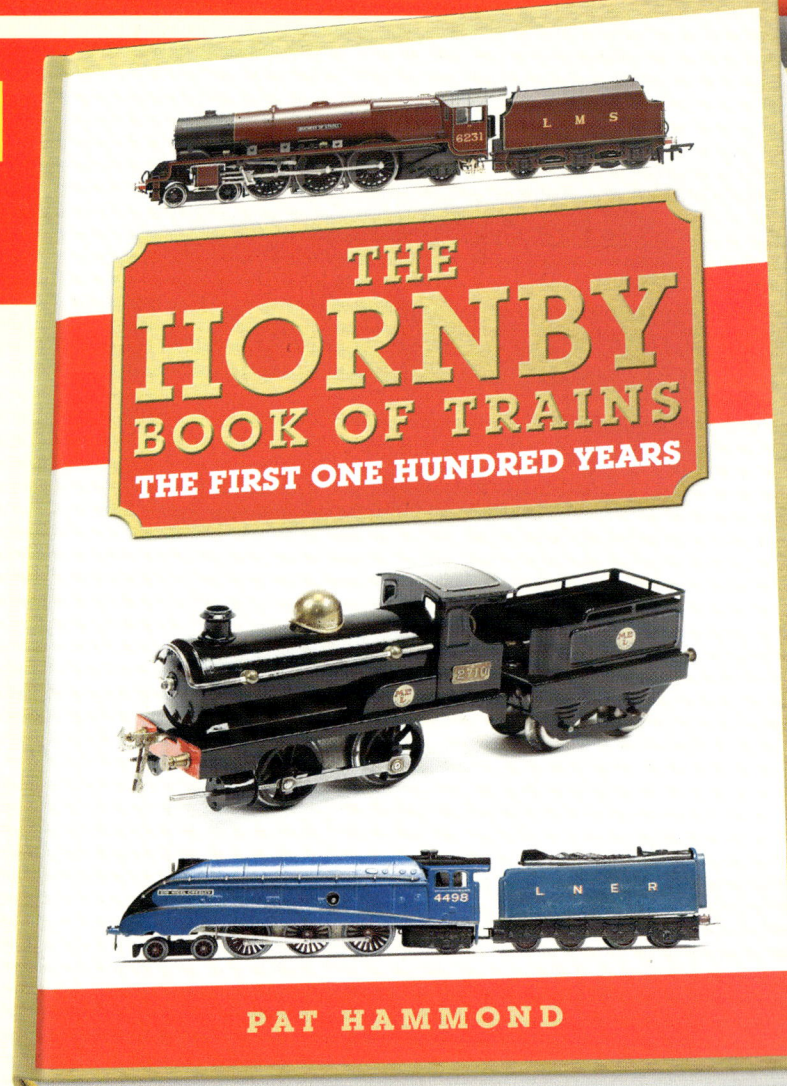

just £25.00

Hardback, 448 pages

This definitive history of Hornby is a must-read for all model railway enthusiasts

LAST FEW COPIES REMAINING
ORDER NOW TO AVOID DISAPPOINTMENT

Free P&P* when you order online at shop.keypublishing.com/hornbybook

OR

Call UK: 01780 480404
Overseas: +44 1780 480404
Monday to Friday 9am-5:30pm GMT

Key Books

HORNBY magazine SUBSCRIBERS CALL FOR YOUR £5.00 DISCOUNT

Viaduct visualisation

Viaduct visualisation

As with many engineering aspects, British Rail had a specialist fleet of vehicles to carry out the examination and maintenance of viaducts, this wagon-based plant having its own support coaches and vans. Trevor Mann describes the development of these viaduct inspection units.

All bridges and viaducts on the British railway network require regular inspection to ensure they remain in a sound condition, not only to rail traffic but also to road users. Many such structures were of course straightforward to check. Bridges passing over the railway, at marginally above the height set by the loading gauge, could be inspected using either ladders or the tunnel inspection vehicles described elsewhere in this volume. Bridges carrying the railway over roads at similar heights could equally easily be accessed using ladders or lightweight scaffolding.

Tall bridges and viaducts, however, posed greater problems as did those over water. Extendable ladders provided access to a greater height but could only reach so far, while boats could be used to examine the piers of river bridges. Sometimes though there was little alternative but to lower an intrepid bridge inspector over the parapet in a cradle.

The Southern Region built a two-vehicle viaduct inspection unit in 1950, this utilising the underframes from EMU stock damaged during wartime. Equipped with mechanical lifting equipment and pulleys, this allowed inspectors to be lowered in a latticework cradle, a solution akin to that still used to clean windows on tall buildings today. Although not condemned until 1964, this was nevertheless something of a false start as all later units used hydraulically powered 'cherry picker' technology.

The original 'Cherry Picker' was invented in California in 1944 initially, as the name suggests, for work in orchards as the operator could manoeuvre the platform to reach the fruit without damaging the tree or returning to the ground to move ladders. Once production began in 1953, the device was soon adapted for use in a range of applications, including installing overhead cables, building maintenance and fire-fighting.

ABOVE: Picture one: Although the photographer was clearly concentrating on the Queen Mary brake van when this view was recorded around 1966, something more exotic lurks beyond! The road vehicle loaded on the Lowmac immediately behind S56302 is a British Railways bridge inspection unit based on a mid-1950s Commer Superpoise. This was an early application of 'cherry picker' technology that almost certainly pre-dated the first of the rail-mounted viaduct inspection units. *Trevor Mann Collection*

Early designs

British Railways was evidently quick to see the potential of the new technology, an early lorry-based bridge inspection unit being illustrated in picture one. Then, in 1957, the North Eastern Region introduced a rail-mounted viaduct inspection unit

Modelling BR Departmental Coaching Stock **109**

Viaduct visualisation

ABOVE: Picture two: DM720014, the second of the pioneering viaduct inspection units built in 1957, is seen on July 27, 1975 en route to Dinting Viaduct, which carried the Woodhead line into the eastern outskirts of Manchester. The cabin at the near end contained a plan table used to record details from the inspection, its occupants being in telephone contact with those in the inspection cradle, while the sheet covered the operating platform and slewing gantry. Peter Fidczuk Collection

ABOVE: Picture three: The view from the opposite end of DM720014, which had become DR82003 during the 1980s, at the Llangollen Railway on May 5, 1993. This nicely illustrates the details of the articulated booms, inspection cradle and operating platform. Other than lettering and the differences inherited from its 'donor' wagon, DE159680 was almost identical but had a window in each cabin side. Hywel Thomas

that was claimed to be the first of its kind in the world. Developed in collaboration with Auto-Mower Engineering and Simon Engineering, this comprised an 'articulated boom lift' mounted on the underframe of ex-LNER 42-ton bogie bolster wagon DE159680.

This pioneering unit, known at least semi-officially as the 'Gozunda', was clearly successful for a second, almost identical, unit entered service with the London Midland Region later the same year. Numbered DM720014 and later DR82003, this converted ex-LMS 35-ton bogie bolster appears in pictures two and three.

When one of these inspection units arrived at a site, a steel rope was anchored to the track some distance in front of and behind the unit. Then, with the inspection team in place, the slewing gantry was rotated through 90 degrees, carrying the operator platform, booms and inspection platform over the parapet. The booms were then deployed, manoeuvring the inspection platform into position for the survey to begin.

The upper boom could be lowered up to 85° below the horizontal and, with that in this near-vertical position, the lower boom was able to travel between 30° above horizontal and 60° below, so allowing inspections to be carried out up to 29 feet below rail level and up to 15 feet inside the face of an arch. When the inspectors needed to inch along the viaduct, they remotely activated a winch on the underframe of the wagon, pulling the vehicle along the wire rope. Diesel engines powered hydraulic pumps that controlled the slewing gantry, booms and winch, and a generator provided electricity for floodlights and the hand tools employed, for example to break out defective masonry or brickwork.

The next two units, very similar in design and operation to those just described, appeared in 1960. Oddly, two rather different wagon types were selected for conversion. As shown in picture 4, DB996262 (later DR82002) was a modified 50-ton Salmon bogie rail wagon initially allocated to the North Eastern Region. Although ten feet longer than the bogie bolsters utilised for the pioneering units, the similarity is obvious. In contrast, DB994001 (DR82001), which was allocated to the Eastern Region, was a converted 40-ton Dolphin rail and sleeper wagon that had a floor almost a foot lower than that on the other units.

More conversions

The next development remains something of a mystery. When it was withdrawn in 1971, the Park Royal DMU featuring Driving Motor Brake Second 50397 and Driving Trailer Composite 56160 was transferred to the Civil Engineers and ear-marked for conversion into a viaduct inspection unit. 50397 was allocated the number DB975137, although this was never applied. It was

ABOVE: Picture four: The viaduct inspection units built in 1961 are exemplified here by DR82002, a conversion of BR 50-ton Salmon DB996262 and photographed at Hitchin on July 20, 1975. Taken from a similar angle to that of picture three, the similarities in design are obvious. Perhaps the most noticeable differences are in the shape and size of the shield at the nearer end and the lack of any covering for the diesel engines and hydraulic pumps immediately behind the operating platform on what would become DR82002. Paul Bartlett

ABOVE: Picture five: Viaduct inspection units invariably ran with a staff coach and tool van, these being progressively modernised over the years. One of those built on a Warwell, DR82101 was stabled at Guide Bridge on March 3, 1988, and accompanied by Vanwide DB782248, this being prominently lettered 'Not to be detached from VIU No 82101' and DB977240, which was a conversion of Mk.1 CCT 94600. Trevor Mann

Viaduct visualisation

ABOVE: **Picture six:** A closer look at a spotless DR82101 on the same day shows the compact nature of the two Warwell-based VIUs with the three operating arms neatly stowing away. The diesel engine was housed in the cabinet at the nearest end while, surprisingly, the original diamond frame bogies remained in place. *Trevor Mann*

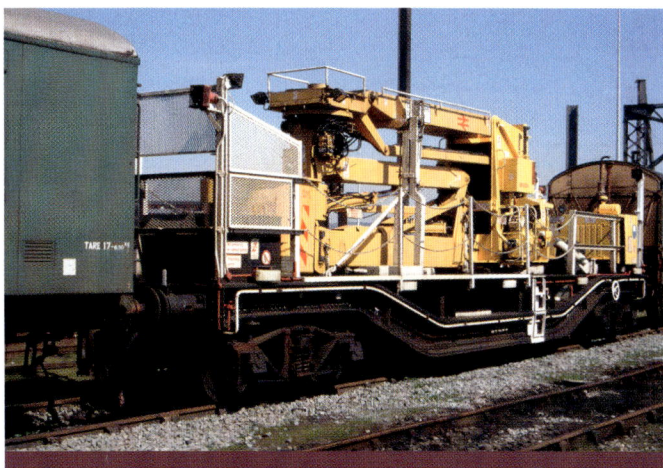

ABOVE: **Picture seven:** Fortuitously, when DR82101 was photographed again, also at Guide Bridge but on April 13. 1995, the other side of the vehicle was facing the sun so it is possible to illustrate both sides and ends. The flat platform on which the gantry unit sat was supported on substantial girder sections running crossways in the former well. *Trevor Mann*

though painted yellow and lettered as 'Chief Civil Engineers Department Universal Viaduct Inspection Unit No.1'. Perversely, 56160 did carry its departmental number of DB975228 but retained BR blue. The set spent some years at Long Rock depot, Penzance, then part-occupied by Liftech Engineering, a firm making 'cherry-picker' lifting gear. However, no further work seems to have been done and photos taken subsequently reveal that even the interior seating remained intact so presumably the project was cancelled.

Returning to the main thread of the story, when the next pair of viaduct inspection units appeared in the late 1970s, they marked a significant advance on the earlier machines. Constructed by Elstree Plant Ltd on Warwell wagons, they incorporated the American-designed TU37 hydraulic lift system. The operating platform was dispensed with and all functions instead controlled from the inspection bucket. There was a turntable instead of a slewing gantry, three articulated booms instead of two, and the final link could extend or retract telescopically. This meant manoeuvrability was greatly improved so there was no longer a need to anchor the machine or to winch it along. Pictures five to seven all illustrate DR82101 which was built on Warwell DM748327 in 1977. The other unit was DR82100, converted in 1975 and mounted on DM748349, which was another Warwell.

Last build
The last viaduct inspection unit to be constructed for British Rail was commissioned in 1980. Built by Armfield Engineering Ltd, this was a conversion of DB901202, a 55-ton Weltrol EJC bogie trolley wagon, which was originally built for services to the continent via the train ferry. The modification took full advantage of the wagon's 71ft length over headstocks to incorporate booms that were much longer than on the Warwell conversions. This enabled the inspection

ABOVE: **Picture nine:** The other side and of DR82201 is seen in this April 26, 1991 view, again taken at Radyr. This shows the size of the engine compartment and also the steps needed for access. With this enormous machine at their disposal, bridge engineers were able to quickly examine a full bridge arch without needing to move the machine. However, despite it being the most modern inspection unit, it was one of the first to be scrapped, this taking place at Crewe in 1997. *Hywel Thomas*

team to examine an area of 2,500 square feet without moving the machine. By telescopically extending the link connected to the inspection platform, it even became possible to examine the far side of a double-track viaduct. Renumbered as DR82201 in the CEPS plant series, this enormous machine is illustrated in pictures eight and nine.

Then, almost as quickly as they had arrived on the scene, they were gone! DE159680 was withdrawn before CEPS numbers were allocated in the mid-1970s, but DM720014, the other pioneering conversion, survived until 1988. Of those introduced in 1961, the Dolphin conversion DB994001 was condemned and scrapped in 1976 but the modified Salmon, renumbered DR82002, lasted into the early 1990s but would then be stored for several years until scrapped in 2000. Initially, both DR82003 and DR82100 found homes in preservation but both were scrapped around 2010. The other pair, DR82101 and DR82201, did not even make the new century as privatisation took effect and new inspection methods were deployed, firstly road/rail vehicles and nowadays drones.

ABOVE: **Picture eight:** The final viaduct inspection unit to be built for British Rail was also the largest, DR82201 utilising the 71ft long Weltrol EJC B901202 as its chassis. This operated throughout England and Wales but not in Scotland, where one of the Warwell conversions was deployed. The vast bulk of the machine is captured at Radyr Yard on April 25, 1992. *Trevor Mann*

Modelling BR Departmental Coaching Stock

Viaduct visualisation

ABOVE: DR82101 dwarfs its two support vans at an unknown location around 1992. The nearest is QPV staff coach DB977239, this being a conversion of a Mk.1 CCT with the end doors completely removed in favour of steel plating, security mesh frames fitted over the windows, one set of doors sealed and the other converted into a single personal door. Gas bottle cabinets are also fitted to the underframe. At the other end of the VIU is ZQX tool van DB889011, this being one of the shorter ferry CCTs and largely unmodified. *Simon Bendall Collection*

ABOVE: Staff and dormitory coach DE321049 stands at Hitchin on an unrecorded date in the mid-1980s while attached to viaduct inspection unit DR82002. Built in 1936, this was a Tourist Third Open to diagram 216 and was assigned to traverse the entire Eastern Region with its machine. Only the underframe survives today after the body was damaged beyond repair by arson in 2000. *Simon Bendall Collection*

ABOVE: A closer look at one of the Mk.1 CCTs modified to work with the VIUs is provided by DB977240 at Guide Bridge on March 29, 1988. The modifications are much the same as sister vehicle DB977239 and were quite lavish in terms of the alterations usually given to ex CCT staff coaches. It still survives today at the Lincolnshire Wolds Railway as a workshop van with none of the alterations reversed. *Trevor Mann*

RIGHT: Similarly, ferry CCT DB889025 was another of its kind to find employment with a VIU as a tool van, this replacing the 12-ton Vanwide that had previously fulfilled this role with DR82101. Seen at Guide Bridge on April 13, 1995, its livery was rather less interesting than the 'Dutch' grey/yellow carried by DB889011 above. Looking rather tired and with flammable Hazchem symbols added, it would be scrapped just a month later. *Trevor Mann*

Viaduct visualisation

A VIU staff coach by Paul Wade

This model of Mk.1 staff, dormitory, and workshop coach DB975534 was built to accompany the viaduct inspection unit scratchbuilt by Steve Farmer and described on the following page. As this was many years ago, I used an old Tri-ang BSK model for this project, working from photographs I had taken at Ashford pre-assembly depot and Tonbridge West Yard.

The coach was broken down into its parts with both sides needing alterations to the door and window layouts. One set of luggage doors was not needed on both sides along with the passenger door next to the guard's door. The windows on these were filled with 40-thou plasticard cut to be a tight fit and as flush to the sides as possible. Filler was then added in any gaps and sanded smooth. The door edges were also filled and sanded with the hinge detail going as well. After priming the body, any further smoothing can then be carried out. Gas heater vents, one on the left side and three on the right, were formed with holes cut out of the body and round vents from slices of rod added with five-thou angled side pieces.

The non-brake end had a shallow plated gangway which was made from 20-thou plasticard profiled to match the pictures. I also added a square box a quarter way up the plated gangway to the left as shown in the photographs. Lamp brackets were made from staples, and holes drilled for the toilet water filler pipes with brass handrail knobs also put in place. The brake end had the gangway completely removed with a ten-thou plasticard rectangle covering the end apart from the top 6mm.

Underframe work
New cast buffers were added after cutting the moulded ones off with the existing battery boxes detailed with Microstrip and two scratchbuilt gas bottle cabinets fitted, these made from 20-thou plasticard and Microstrip. Steps on the solebars were needed under the doors with an extra step under the guard's doors with staples used to fix them to the chassis floor. Whitemetal handbrake levers from my scrap box were added to both sides.

On the roof, ridged dome cast roof vents replaced the moulded ones and water filler pipes were made from 0.5mm brass wire with the top made from a slice of a 2mm round sprue. The guard's doors had handrails added with brass handles and grabrails on the other doors.

The body was painted with Humbrol No.76 green with some small patches of olive green from the previous faded livery where the old writing and numbers were retained.

Internally, curtains were provided while all the glazing was covered in Hurst Models mesh-effect plastic sheet on the inside to represent the wire grilles added over the windows. Finally, the transfers were mostly separate letters and numbers with the toilet window painted in a dirty white.

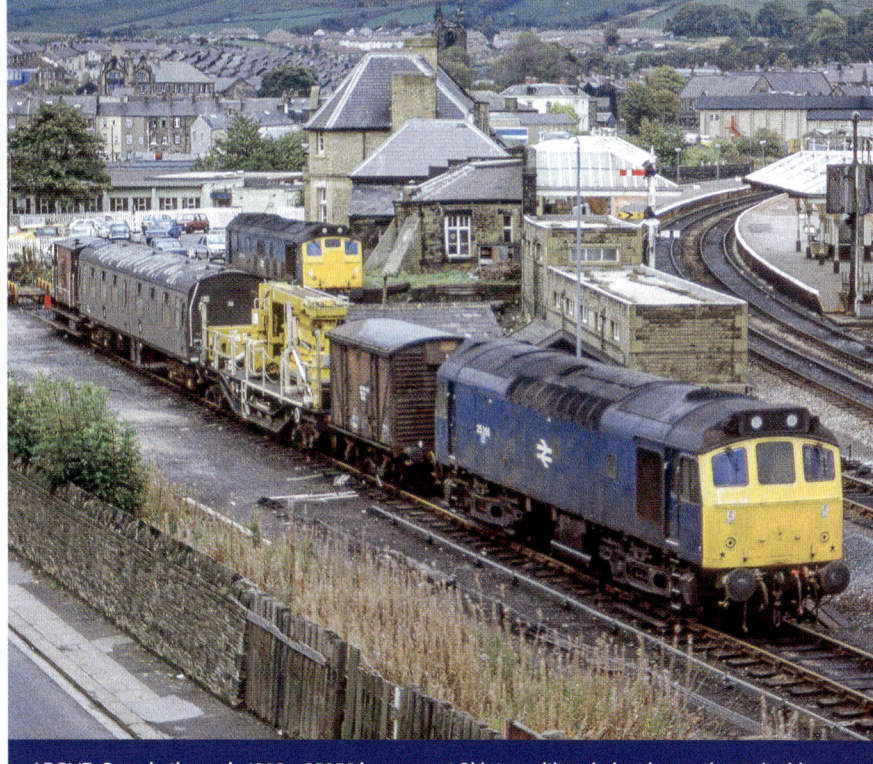

ABOVE: Seen in the early 1980s, 25256 lays over at Skipton with a viaduct inspection unit, this featuring one of the Warwell-based units, DR82100 or DR82101. Accompanying it are the obligatory tool van, a Vanwide in this case, a BR brake van on the rear and a Mk.1 staff coach. While this is a former second class vehicle rather than a BSK, it has received many of the same alterations, including removed gangways, gas bottle cabinets and sealed doors. Simon Bendall Collection

Modelling BR Departmental Coaching Stock 113

Viaduct visualisation

A Warwell-based VIU by Steve Farmer

This 4mm scale model of a viaduct inspection unit was built over 20 years ago after seeing photos of such vehicles published in magazines. Destined for use on Tonbridge West Yard, it was based on DR82100 and assembled using only photographs and a basic line diagram for reference. By necessity it was a compromise as it is only in recent years that a model of the correct Warwell wagon has become available, so this utilises a modified Mainline GWR 'Crocodile' as its base.

All the components for the wagon were scratchbuilt from a mix of Plastruct and Slater's plastic strip and sheet with brass wire used for items like the handrails. Although daunting, if you treat it as a series of elements and take one at a time, it becomes easier. First the deck was constructed with plastic section used to represent the steel beams in the well, these being glued in place and giving a flat surface on which to build. The turntable base was built next followed by the tower section and then the upper arm. Some time was spent on getting this first arm correct as if it was too long or short, it would ruin the overall look of the model.

The other two arms could then be built using photos and sizing them against the first one and the space available between it and the deck. The operator's bucket was again made from plastic and, if I remember correctly, used about eight individual pieces all filed into shape and built up a piece at a time. Once this was done, the basic structure of the VIU was complete and I could then go back and build up the detail.

The engine and hydraulic unit was again built from plastic and based on the reference photos. The handrails and lighting posts were assembled from the brass wire and glued in place with some 40 links per inch chain used for the removable sections on the side. All the various sub-assemblies were then painted, mostly using Humbrol yellow, and assembled on top of the wagon, which had also been painted in preparation. All the transfers came from the Fox range and largely involved applying individual characters. Once done, light weathering was added followed by a coat of matt varnish. I was certainly happy with the results, and it conveys the look of a VIU even if not fully accurate.